THE INSANITY OF HUMANITY

'Dipo Toby Alakija

ISBN: 978 - 36348 - 6 - 0
978-978-36348-6-2
Printed By

Published by the publishing house of

CALVARY ROCK RESOURCES

19, Ajina Street, Ikenne Remo,
Ogun State,
Nigeria.

36, Thomson road
Gorton
Manchester
M18 7QQ
United Kingdom

270 Madison Avenue
Suite 1500, New York, NY 10016
United States

www.calvaryrock.org

INTRODUCTION OF WORLD POWER BROKERS

With series of case studies, especially that of America, humanity can be proved to be deceived, brainwashed and almost at the brink of insanity. Through ideologies, chains of events, financial and other establishments; the world power brokers know and are doing exactly what needs to be done to subject all humans into their control.

As an introduction and way to understand the workings of these world brokers that would later be considered as world secret government, there is need to first study the case of the Us President who was bold enough to challenge these power brokers. But he paid dearly for it with his life.

Through studies of series of works of researchers on the assassination of John F. Kennedy, the result of the findings of Wes Penre is noteworthy because it seems to portray a deeper understanding of the secrets behind the cause of his death and that of his brother and son.

Extract from Wes Penre's article which is titled: 'The Assassination Of John F. Kennedy And The Reserve Bank' may serve as the main introduction of the world power brokers. It thus goes:

"Since that dreadful day on November 22nd of 1963 when JFK was assassinated, there has been lots of speculations as to why and by whom he was murdered. You may think you have heard it all, and that you don't need another theory. However, I have researched JFK quite a bit; especially with regards to the assassination, and I have come up with a different, and not widely discussed possibility for the killing, with a parallel that goes back almost a hundred years in time.

"JFK was a very controversial President; he wanted to change things around. By doing so, you can't please everyone, and he stepped on quite a few toes. One thing he wanted to do was to reorganize the CIA from within, because he considered the Agency being a Government, within the Government, with too much power. Allen Dulles, who was one of the heads of CIA at the time did not like the idea and this alone could have been the reason for the assassination. But there is another interesting aspect as well...

1

"To understand this theory we must understand that the real power is not with the politicians, but with the International Bankers (and ultimately those whom are behind them in this complex web of power). Whomever is running the show use banking and finance as their most powerful tool to accomplish their goals. You and I can try to run for Presidency if we want to, but we would not stand much of chance. It is not because we don't have good ideas, or are capable enough, but we don't have the right super rich sponsors. The final candidates are the ones that are chosen by the International Bankers and sponsored by them. The rest of the candidates cannot afford to compete. Also, the same sponsors support both parties, and can therefore keep almost total control over the election.

"Most people know that the FEDERAL Reserve bank is creating the US dollars. But the truth is that the Federal Reserve is not federal at all, but owned by twelve super wealthy International Banking families, such as the Rothschild's and the Rockefellers. This is a well hidden secret, but can even be verified in 'Encyclopedia Britannica'...

"What JFK did was to create interest-free government money, backed up by the silver reserve, contrary to the Federal Reserve money, which is not backed up by anything. He wanted to pay off the US debt this way. Apparently aware of th secret behind the Federal Reserve, he decided to go back and follow the Constitution. Of course, this was a very dangerous thing to do, because if he was allowed, it could put the International Bankers out of business in the long run. So this was even more serious than to reorganize the CIA.

"Interestingly enough, soon after the assassination the interest-free money was taken out of circulation...

"May be the assassination of President Kennedy was a warning to successors not to make the same 'mistake' as this courageous President did. Brilliance is only allowed and acknowledged if it serves the Illuminati Agenda. Although Mr Kennedy was of Illuminati bloodline and probably also an occultist on some level, and even involved in practices common men would disagree with, I believe he was a man of honour when it came to politics and he took his job very seriously. Being a Kennedy (Illuminati Bloodline) was enough for the International Bankers to sponsor him, thinking he would adjust to the Agenda, especially when his mob related father, Joe Kennedy,

2

fought hard to get his son into the office. Joe was in great favour with the Illuminati pins. But time told them they made a mistake and put a person in power whom refused to abide and had his own ideas, eager to execute them.

"The same thing goes for his brother Robert, and his son John F. Kennedy Jr., who threatened to reveal the Secret Behind Power shortly before he had his "accident". It is very interesting to see that all these three Kennedy's are now dead before their time, while Edward (Ted) Kennedy is still alive, being the one who goes in father Joe's footsteps to bring the New World Order into a reality..."

With Wes Penre's observations about Federal Reserve Bank who creates US dollar notes and being owned by twelve super wealthy International Banking families whom he suspects as members of the Illuminati, we probably understand the reason the US 1 dollar bill has Illuminati logo on it.

With this brief, we take a journey deeper into the study of what is bringing about the Insanity Of Humanity.

CHAPTER ONE

<u>SECRET GOVERNMENT AND THE AGENTS OF CONTROL</u>

Benjamin Disraeli said, "Governments do not govern but merely control the machinery of government, being themselves controlled by the hidden hand."

Mark Twain also said, "we are all ignorant just about different things."

Unknown to most people all over the world, there are various agents at various levels and capacities that are trying to take control of the whole world. These agents had been working for centuries, ranging from one generation right into another with the insane determination to succeed and come about the New Order Of The World. According to the findings of various research works, these agents of control which John Todd dubbed as Secret Government is responsible for various revolutions, world wars and assassinations of many world leaders.

Buggerlugz whose source of information is the top Illuminati defector, John Todd, says, "Grand Druid council of 13 witches rule with Rothschilds as Secret Government... The Illuminati is a vast, highly organized and powerful occult conspiracy that holds mankind in a satanic vice." He says that the Illuminati are thousands of different conspiracies operating in parallels. For example, their vows and initiation rites closely mirror freemasonry.

Now the question is: who exactly is John Todd and why should we believe him or the story about the New World Order?

John Todd also known as John Todd Collins or Lance Collins was one of first former members of the Illuminati in the late 1970s who began a series of speaking engagements at various evangelical churches and organizations. He said his mission was to expose the workings and plans of the Illuminati. He was a high level member before he became a Christian in 1972.

He warned people about the plans for the world domination before he was framed and effectively discredited. The words he left on his audio tapes are still coming to fulfillment. This, of course, put lots of credibility on his claims and proves the fact that he was an insider. The audio tapes speak about the evil plans of the Illuminati to control the world, which explains what is going on in the world today.

John Todd left the illuminati when he became a Christian but before then, he ruled a 13-state US region, consisting of 500 covens, making 65,000 priests and priestesses under him. These are just ministers, not the congregation.

Skeptics say that if the Illuminati were real, there would be defectors. According to Buggerlugz, there are plenty of defectors, clinics that deal with victims of CIA mind control and satanic visual abuse. The vocal ones get put away. And so in 1987, John Todd was framed for rape and sentenced to 30 years imprisonment. According to Fritz Springmeier, when Todd was freed in 1994, he was picked up by a helicopter and murdered. There was a record of Todd being released from prison in South Carolina in April 2004 and then being re-incarcerated in the "Behavioural Disorder Treatment Unit" of the South Carolina Department of mental health.

Todd has provided many shocking revelations, which Fritz Springmeier confirms could only come from a man who was in fact a member of the council of thirteen. Fritz explains that the 13 Illuminati families consist of "generational Satanists."

Todd revealed that the Rothschilds top the Illuminati hierarchy. He leads the Illuminati and in every country, they have a family. In the United States, David Rockefeller is both the head of the Council of Foreign Relations and the Trilateral (commission) which is the name of the Illuminati within the United States. According to him, on top of each pyramid, the Illuminati logo, there is a capstone with an eye in it. The capstone is the Rothschild family Tribunal that rules the Illuminati. The eye is Lucifer, their god and their voice. The first 3 top blocks are on every pyramid. The top block is what John Todd was initiated into which is the council of 13 called Grand Druid council. They only take order from the Rothschilds and nobody else. The council of 33 is directly under the 13. They are the 33 highest Masons in the world. The council of 500, is made up of some of the richest people and conglomerates in the world.

Even as part of the set up of world government, John Todd said he always had his doubt that the secret agenda was ever going to be successfully carried out until a letter that was sent to the council of 13 from London, indicating the plan for world take over. It was revealed in the letter that a man who was believed to be the son of Lucifer had been found.

Todd explained that the take-over plan involved economic breakdown where even Illuminati companies went broke. He further said that, as in the Bolsherik and French Revolutions, millions will be killed in a helter-skelter, which will mark the beginning of reign of terror. According to him, the only thing deterring this plan is widespread gun ownership among the US population. He also talked about some music which is designed to cast a demonic spell on the listener but this will be a subject of discussion under the tools of mind control. What is instructive to note in the revelation of John Todd is that there is a secret government who is trying to use every means to control the world.

He revealed that the Illuminati has found the son of Lucifer who is to be used to pave way for the execution of the secret agenda of the secret government. While skeptic may question the authenticity of these revelations, no one can deny the fact that various bills that are being enacted or presented by the US government like the health care and the gun control bills all substantiate the revelation of John Todd in 1980s. There are so many other events in history, including the French Revolution, world 1 and 2 which point out the fact that there is indeed a secret Government that is working tirelessly to take over the world, ranging from one generation to another, using all kinds of warfare to ensure that the world is reduced into one small community.

CHAPTER TWO

THE ACT OF BRAINWASHING AND MIND CONTROL

Edward Hunter, author of "Brainwashing in Red China" said in 1958 before a US congressional House committee, "since man began, he has tried to influence other men or women to his way of thinking. There have always been these forms of pressure to change attitudes. We discovered in the past thirty years, a technique to influence by clinical, hospital procedures, the thinking processes of human beings. Brainwashing is formed out of a set of different elements... hunger, fatigue, tenseness, threats, violence, and in more intense cases drugs and hypnotism."

The act of Brainwashing and mind control can be performed in various ways with various means, ranging from trauma to monarch mind control but this chapter will only treat the ways of mass mind control and mild or subtle brainwashing.

Toping the list of mass mind control is the media.

MASS MEDIA

This is the most powerful tool used by the controlling class to hypnotize or manipulate the masses. It shapes and molds opinions and attitudes.

Mass media are designed to reach the largest audience possible. They include the use of television, music, movies, radio, newspapers, magazines, books, records, video games and the internet. Many studies have been conducted in the past century to measure the effects of mass media on the population in order to discover the best techniques to enhance it. From these studies emerged the Science of Communication which is used in marketing, public relations and politics.

According to analysts, there are a growing number of people waking up to the reality of our growing transparent soft cage. There seems to be just enough people who choose to remain asleep. Worse yet, there are even those who were at least partially awake at one time but found it necessary to return to the slumber of dreamland, which is created by the mass media.

One of the most common examples of mind control with the use of media in America, being our case study, is the so-called "free and civilized society" in the advent and usage of television set. Although, of course, this does not mean that everything on TV is geared towards brainwashing or mind control but most of the programming on television today all over the world is run and programmed by the largest media corporations that have interests in defense contracts such as CBS, NBC, FOX and a host of others. This makes perfect sense when you see how slanted and warped the news is today. When the conflicts of interest are examined, it would be discovered that the issue is only viewed at a glance. To understand the multiple ways how lies become truths, you only need to examine the techniques of brainwashing, which the network are employing.

Radio is not different in the ability to brainwash a population into submission. About sixty-seven years ago, six million Americans became unwitting subjects in an experiment in psychological warfare. It was the night before Halloween in 1938. At 8 p.m CST, the Mercury Radio on the Air began broadcasting Orson Welles' radio adaptation of H.G Wells' War Of The Worlds. The story was presented as if it were breaking news, with bulletins so realistic that an estimated one million people believed the world was actually under attack by Martians. Of that number, thousands succumbed to outright panic, not waiting to hear Welles' explanation at the end of the program that it had all been a Halloween prank, but fleeing into the night to escape the alien invaders.

Psychologist Hadley Cantril in his book: The Invasion From Mars: A Study In The Psychology Of Panic, explored the power of broadcast media, particularly as it relates to the suggestibility of human beings under the influence of fear. Cantril was affiliated with Princeton University's Radio Research project, which was funded in 1937 by the Rockefeller Foundation. Also affiliated with the project was Council on Foreign Relations (CFR) member and Columbia Broadcasting System (CBS) Executive Frank Stanton. Station was the chairman of the board of Rand Corporation, the influential think tank which has done ground breaking research on, among other things, mass brainwashing. With Rockefeller Foundation money, Cantril established the Office of Public

Opinion Research (OPOR). Among the studies conducted by OPOR was an analysis of the effectiveness of "psycho-political operations" (which means propaganda in plain English) Of office of Strategic Services (OSS), the forerunner of the Central Intelligence Agency (CIA). During world war 2, Cantril with Rockefeller's money assisted CFR member and CBS reporter Edward R Murrow in setting up Princeton radio propaganda Listening Centre with the purpose of studying Nazi radio propaganda with the object of applying Nazi techniques to OSS propaganda. Out of this project came a new government agency called Foreign Intelligence Service (FBIS). The FBIS eventually became the United State Information Agency (USIA), which is the propaganda arm of the National Security Council. Thus, by the end of the 1940s, the basic research had been done and the propaganda apparatus of the national security state had been set up just in time for the Dawn of Television.

Experiments conducted by researcher Herbert Krugman reveals that when a person watches television, brain activity switches from the left to the right hemisphere. The left hemisphere is the scat of logical thought. This is where information is broken down into its component parts and critically analyzed. The right brain, however, treats incoming data uncritically, processing information in wholes, leading to emotional, rather than logical responses. The shift from left to right brain activity also causes the release of endorphin, body's natural opiates - thus it is possible to become physically addicted to watching television, a hypothesis borne out of numerous studies which has shown that very few people are able to kick the television habit. It is no longer an overstatement to note that most youths today that are raised and taught through network television are intellectually dead by their early teens.

The dumbing down of humanity is represented by another shift which occurs in the brain when we watch television. Activity in the higher brain regions (such as the neo-cortex) is diminished, while activity system increases. The latter, commonly referred to as the reptile brain, is associated with more primitive mental functions, such as the "fight" or "fright" response. The reptile brain is unable to distinguish between reality and the pretended reality of television. To the reptile brain, if it looks real, it is real. Thus, though we know on a conscious level that it is "only a film," and yet, for instance, the heart beats faster while we watch a suspenseful scene. Similarly, we know the commercial is trying to manipulate us, but on an unconscious level, the commercial nonetheless succeeds in, say, making us feel inadequate until we buy whatever is being advertised. The effect is all the more powerful because it is unconscious, operating on the deepest level of human response. The reptile brain, however, makes it possible for us to survive as biological beings, but it also leaves people vulnerable to the manipulations of television programmers. This is where the manipulators use our own emotions as strings to control us. The distortions and directions we are being moved to are taking place in the subconscious, often undetected.

The above is the submission of results of research works of analysts of how the mass media can be used as a way to hypnotize or manipulate the masses. This result is able shed light on why the whole world is being manipulated by the secret government to a large extent.

CHAPTER THREE

PROPAGANDA TECHNIQUES OF BRAINWASHING

The most dangerous way to dehumanize humanity is to brainwash them or control their minds. Propaganda, especially through media is one of the most effective ways to brainwash people.

Propaganda techniques were first codified and applied in a scientific manner by journalist Walter Lippman and psychologist Edward Bernays in early 20th century. During world war 1, Lippman and Bernays were hired by the then United States President to participate in the Creel Commission. Their mission was to sway popular opinion in favour of entering the war, on the side of Britain. Edward Bernays said in his book in 1928, "The conscious and intelligent manipulation of the organized habits and opinions of the masses is an important element in democratic society. Those who manipulate this unseen mechanism of the society constitute an invisible government, which is the true ruling power of our country."

The Creed Commission became so unpopular that after the war, Congress closed it down without providing funding to organize and archive its papers. However, the war propaganda campaign of Lippman and Bernays produced such an intense anti-German hysteria within six months. Barnays coined the terms "group mind" and "engineering consent," as important concepts in practical propaganda work. The current public relations industry, according to analyst, is a direct outgrowth of Lippman's and Bernay's work, which is still in use extensively by the United States government.

Word War II saw continued use of propaganda as a weapon of war, both by Hitler's propagandist, Joseph Gobbles and the British political warfare Executive as well as the United States office of war information.

As Edward Hunter has stated that brainwashing is formed out of set of different elements like hunger, fatigue, tenseness, threats, violence, the techniques of propaganda are increasingly becoming sophisticated over the time as the mind scientists continue to discover scientific breakthroughs as to how the human brain functions, learns, retains information and behaves. The most effective brainwashing techniques are used on the most successful propaganda networks. Like the monkey that is attracted to shiny objects, when there is proper amount of glamour, the propaganda catches attention of the people. The unimaginable fallacies are created as truths, not because it is logical but because of the broken record technique. No matter how ridiculous the lie, if it is repeated enough, the brain does not know the difference between reality and fiction. This techniques is underestimated in its ability to allow the puppeteers to hypnotize millions of people. Hollywood will continue to frighten the people with films on gangsters, wars and the corrupt blue collar criminal. In the end, the programers already influence the people to make up their minds. This is because they see it on TV, read it on the newspapers, hear it on radio and saw it on several movies the need to give more powers to dictate to their lives. According to David L. Robb, author of Operation Hollywood, "Hollywood and the Pentagon have a long history of making movies together. It is a tradition that stretches back to the early days of silent films, and extends right up until the present day. It's been a collaboration that works well for both sides. Hollywood producers get what they want - access to billions of dollars worth of military hardware and equipments - tanks, jet fighters, nuclear submarines and aircraft carriers - and the military gets what it wants - films that portray the military in a positive light; films that help the services in the recruiting efforts. The Pentagon is not merely a passive supporter of films, however. If the Pentagon doesn't like a script, it will usually suggest script changes that will allow the film to receive the military's support and approval. Sometimes these proposed changes are minor. But sometimes the changes are dramatic. Sometimes they change dialogue. Sometimes they change characters. Sometimes they even change history. They create something coined "disinfortainment". They mix disinformation with entertainment and call it disinfotainment.

The unadulterated violence is now accepted on regular TV with sharp shooters, bombers and assassins being worshiped if they are fighting for the system. This odd reality transfers itself into the shady world of video games that stepped in plots and tasks to kill as much as the player can. The players are getting younger and younger with 7 out of 10 children playing games with a mature rating. Children today are being indoctrinated through their favorite games and law enforcement programs to push buttons of the weapons of mass destruction for tomorrow's world.

With the use of these techniques, people's minds are geared towards conformity, ignoring diversity. Network programming, whether it is news or dramas, is geared towards artificially creating your world and reality. With proper amount of entertainment and sensationalism people may be living their lives through the television set. Many anchors and actors are beautiful and research indicates that attractive people are often perceived as trust worthy.

The propaganda techniques with the use of the media is being used to take the power to exercise the free will of humanity. Through the experiment that was conducted by Herbert Krugman, we see that the seat of the logical thoughts, where information is broken down into it's component parts for critical analysis is made almost dormant. By constantly using the region which is referred to as the reptile brain, the human brain is programmed through fake world that is created in movies and other form of entertainments. That is the reason the people, especially the youths and children are being characterized with foul language, immoralities, crimes and violence. Contrary to what used to be, many people no longer value human lives. The people who had been brainwashed through the media to go for gold at the expense of human lives, dress and act like animals at the expense of moral values. These brainwashed people are now the ones designing the entire world system. The world system makes the people think alike, which is one of the first step the secret government needs to do before making them collective herd with no minds of their own.

Brainwashing through the media had victimized hundreds of million if not billions of people all over the world. Waking up the victims from their dreamland or switching over the seat of the logical thoughts from the region of reptile brain is proving to be a masculine task. If you are a victim, you need to help yourself analysis the state of the world by yourself. This compilation of results of research works of researchers is aimed at exposing the truth about what is been done to humanity.

CHAPTER FOUR

<u>BRAINWASHING THROUGH EDUCATION</u>

Rick Santorum revealed that American colleges brainwash students, making home schooling more important in the present days.

Raymond Houghton said, "...absolute behaviour control is imminent."

According to analysts, conforming the masses to a particular way of thinking requires all the sophisticated tools and tactics which had been developed at the various "behavioural science research institutes. Education laboratories were established first in England, then in the Soviet Union and Nazi Germany, and finally in the United States. Going by the battles of these psycho-social engineers against an unsuspecting public, they would "wash" away individual thinking, free speech and all the other rights of Americans and other people in the world. The vacuum would be filled with lofty ideals, enticing images and deceptive promises designed to mold minds that match their global vision. Group thinking and other controls and incentives would enforce compliance.

A well known story which bombards children with mind-changing suggestions was narrated to first-graders in America. It typically illustrates both the tactics and the planned transformation of the world.

The story is about the little Red Hen who wanted to eat some bread. She asked some of her barnyard friends to help her in making it. The cat, the dog and the goat all said, "no". She decided to do all the work herself. When the bread was done, its fragrance spread through out the farm; her neighbours who were unwilling to bake the bread with her were willing to help her eat it.

"Wont you share with us?" they begged.

"No," the Red Hen said. "Since you didn't help you don't get anything."

In the context of traditional values, the moral lesson in the story is clear: you get nothing from what you don't work for. The story is intended to promote active work and discourage laziness. But those who have learned to think and see from the new global view are led to a different conclusion. The kinds of questions the first grade teacher asks her class is: "why was the little Red Hen so stingy? Isn't it only right that everyone gets to eat? Why wouldn't she share what she had with some who had none?"

The concerned mother who heard and reported this story asked, "what kind of values were the children taught?"

The obvious answer to this question of the mother is children were being taught socialist values. The teacher's question was actually strategic suggestions, prompting the group to ridicule traditional values, to see reality and society from the new politically correct perspective, and to shame anyone who dare to disagree.

The educational establishment knows that children who are fed with traditional values or biblical principles will resist the plans for change. The system recognizes the fact that students bombarded with strategic suggestions and idealized images will likely reject Christianity and other values. If schools can build the right kind of framework of filter in the minds of children early enough, the new global beliefs will fit right in. In other words, the battle for the hearts and minds of children will be won by the side that first trains them to see reality from its point of view.

Aldous Huxley, author of "Brave New World" proves that he understands these concepts well when he wrote that education must provide a mental framework... within which any piece of information acquires in the later life may find its proper and significant place.

The global vision is well pronounced in the basic goal of UNESCO's worldwide program for "life long learning" and summarized in "Our Creative Diversity," the 1995 book-sized report from the United Nation Commission on Culture and Development. It says, "The challenge to humanity is to adopt new ways of thinking, new ways of acting, new ways of living."

The implication of implementing this basic goal is to wash away through education whatever form of culture, religion, values or the belief you stand for and then instill the new ways of life and belief into the minds of individuals.

There is a case study of a single mother who has seven children that establish this fact.

One of the children who was a girl of about six years old started going to school one day. She found out that the teacher would not allow her to pray over her lunch as her mother have taught her.

The mother who did not even have a high school diploma pulled her out of school to home-school her and other children. This was the time home-schooling was not as popular as it is in US. Back then, it was not official either and it was a subject of harassment from the school. The school bus would sit outside and lay on the horn every morning. The bus driver would yell, "truant" and sometimes even get out, going to bang the door. The school call all the time, and the mother stopped answering the phone.

One day, the mother got what she feared for a long time - an official letter saying she had to go to court for her daughter's truancy. She was dazed as she read the letter. She couldn't believe what she read, letting the letter fall out of her hand in despair. The daughter went to her and asked her if it was bad news. She said, "yes". She asked if she could read the letter. Since it was about her, she let her read the letter. Without her mother noticing it right away, the 6-year old girl got a red pen and began to circle several grammatical and spelling errors in the letter. Her mother scolded her, saying she wasn't supposed to do that to other people's papers. But then, the mother had done that to the girl's papers over times. So it was the mother that taught her at home.

When the mother went to court, taking the letter with her to make sure she went to the right place, she was bought before the judge. The Judge asked her if she knew why she was in the court. She handed him the letter, forgetting about the markings. She was almost certain that he would ask her a bunch of questions about her own education and concluded that she was unfit to home-school her daughter. He would, according to her conclusion, order her to take her daughter back to school.

When the judged looked at the letter, he asked, "who put these markings on here?"

With apology, the mother told him it was the daughter in question.

The judge took off his glasses and looked at the letter again. He said to her, "well, the reason you're here today is that it is suspected that your daughter is not being properly educated. However, it appears that she is being educated, and from what I see here, it is clearly not coming from the public schools. This case is dismissed."

The mother did not realize that she had seen teaching her daughter 7th grade reading level instead of 1st grade.

This case indicates the fact that so many schools are established to show more interest in washing away traditional values and impacting global vision than in academics.

CHAPTER FIVE

BRAINWASHING THROUGH DRUGS

In his article on March 3, 2011, Vaughan Bell talked about a scary brainwashing drug called Burundanga, relating the news report from Ecuador that year about a motorist who recalled that he was approached by two women and lost consciousness. After waking up, he discovered that his car and possession were all gone. The news report also indicated that a girl in Venezuela came round in the hospital to discover that she had been abducted and sexually assaulted in Colombia. Customers of a street vendor were robbed after eating spiked food. Each of these had been doped with Burundanga, an extract of the Brugmansia plant containing high levels of the psychoactive chemical scopolamine.

The scale of the problem in Latin America is not known, but a recent survey of emergency hospital in Bogota, Colombia, found that around 70 per cent of patients drugged with Burundanda had also been robbed, and around three percent assaulted. According to Juliana Gomez, a Colombian psychiatrist who treats victims of Burundanga poisoning, the most common symptoms are confusion and amnesia. It makes victims disoriented and sedated so they can be easily robbed. Medical evidence verifies this. News reports indicate that the drugs removes freewill effectively, turning victims into suggestible human puppets. Although not fully understood by neuroscience as at the time of reporting, freewill is seen as a highly complex neurological ability and one of the most cherished of human characteristics. Clearly, if a drug can eliminate this, it highlights a stark vulnerability at the core of our species.

Medical science is yet to establish if the drug affects our autonomy, but it is known that scopolamine affects memory and makes people more passive.

Neuroscientist Renate Thienel from the University of Newcastle in Australia has studied it effects on problem-solving and memory tasks during brain scans. He notes that "scopolamine has selective effects on memory, although other mental functions such as planning and information and manipulation are unaffected." This invariably suggests victims remain cognitively nimble but unable to retain information.

The key seems to be that scopolamine blocks acetylcholine, a neurotransmitter essential to memory. Scans also reveal that the drug affects the amygdala, a brain area controlling aggression and anxiety. This would explain scopolamine's pacifying effect. Evidence also suggests victims tend to be confused and passive rather than unable to resist command yet until scopolamine's role in the chemistry of freewill is fully explored, we can only speculate that the criminal underworld has unwittingly stumble upon one of the greatest discoveries of 21st - century neuroscience.

Another article, in fact a research work on the same drug was made by Ryan Duffy Vice who went to Colombia to find out about the drug with the slang "Zombie drug". The drug was actually scopolamine or burudanga.

According to Vice's discovery, it was a hazardous drug that eliminates freewill, capable of wiping out the memory of its victims.

Vice interviewed drug dealers and asked those who have fallen victim, Demencia Black said the drug is frightening for the simplicity in which it can be administered. He told Vice that scopolamine can be blown in the face of a passer-by on the street, and within minutes, that person is under the drug's effect. Scopolamine is odorless and tasteless.

Black said, "you can guide them where you want. It's like they're a child."

A Colombian woman who was a victim said that under the influence of scopolamine, she led a man to her house and helped him ransack it. According to the drugs dealer, the drug turns people into a complete zombie and blocks memories from forming. So even after the drug wears off, victims have no recollection as to what happened.

According to the British journal of clinical pharmacology, the drug - also knows as hyoscine - causes the same level of memory loss as diazepam. In ancient times, the drug was given to the mistresses of dead Colombian leaders and told to enter their mater's grave, where they were buried alive.

In modern times, the CIA used the drug as a tool of cold war interrogations, with the hope of using it like a truth serum.

However, because of the drug's chemical make-up, it also induces powerful hallucinations.

A woman called Nicky in Puerto Rico said that the plant (scopolamine) does not grow only in South America. Since she was a kid her father had a farm in Puerto Rico where the tree grew wildly. In the 80s when she was a teenager, her cousin went to visit and got a little excited because Nicky's father had so many in his 5 acres farm. He explained that when the leaves are boiled and made into tea, it would induce a very "high note" after it is drunk. It would last for hours. The plant which was commonly used instead of other illegal drugs is called "Te de campana" (bells tea). After he heard about the dangerous drugs, Nicky's father ordered his farm employees to immediately get rid of the trees. Later in life, Nicky found out that many of the teens that drank the tea suffered health complications, brain damage, memory loss and even deaths.

With cases of mental problems on the increase in every nation, one cannot help but to trace the major cause to the use of drugs to brainwash people as evidenced in the above cases. The havoc which had been done to human brains through the use of drugs like marijuana, cannabis, Indian helm, cocaine, heroine and a host of others, including the legal and the illegal ones can never be quantified. It not only increases the number of mental patients in mad houses but also increases the crime rate all over the world. By encouraging the use of drugs that alter the functions of human brains, the agent of control plan to erase diversity, bringing about conformity and or turning man into machines they can control with drugs or buttons.

CHAPTER SIX

BRAINWASHING THROUGH ENTERTAINMENT

With reference to the experiments by Herbert Krugmane which was treated in chapter two, when a person watches television, brain activity switches from the seat of logical thoughts to the reptile brain which is unable to distinguish the reality and the assumed reality or fiction. In essence, a well fabricated story that is packaged especially in movies, can really influence or hypnotize the audience. Hence, fake life in movies can be taken as real life. Right from childhood, people are brainwashed with cartoons they watch on TV. The owners of mega huge entertainment industries like Walt Disney are members these agencies of brainwashing. They have so many demonic and subliminal messages in the majority of cartoons which children are fond of watching. The movies and the so-called reality show like American or Nigerian idol or whatever they call it are designed to pass subliminal messages. These messages are hardly recognized by conscious mind but in most, if not all cases, affect the way of thinking or the sub conscious mind. Often times, after the messages had been registered into the brain, they come into the minds and without knowing the source, the human mind begin to act on it. The movies and TV shows create fantasies that make the audience think that this is how life should be. Sometimes you wonder how someone can command thunder without using supernatural forces in a movie, making it appear like a natural gift. Before the audience knows it, they begin to aspire to acquire the power even if it is demonic. The subliminal message in that kind of movies is that the audience can possess the power through whatever means they choose. How about the so-called-reality show that makes people live their lives through the contestants, making you to feel that you can be an idol too? Most people behind reality show are puppets of occultists or are in secret cults.

In subliminal messages in movies, TV, music and other forms of entertainments, witchcraft or magic or cult powers are introduced to audience. Sometimes it may be in the form of pictures or coded words. The use of hypnotism kind of method that make audience switch from the seat of logical thoughts to the reptile brain is common in most of the entertainments. While it must be admitted that it is not all the entertainments that carry the message that is meant to brainwash the audience, it must be emphasized that most of the dramas, music, information and even news are scripted with the intention to brainwash the people or to introduce witchcraft, magic, cult powers, trauma, and all sorts of things into their minds and then hold them captive.

Probably out of feelings of success in many reality shows, MTV which used to be music TV some years ago is now full of reality shows that are wasting away audience time in entertainment brainwash. The entertainments nowadays not only wash away the things that really make life meaningful but also teach so many youths and children to drink, take drugs, mess around like street dogs and even kill themselves. A typical example of this occurred in America few years ago when a child whose favourite star in a movie killed himself by hanging. The child also went to hang himself.

The entertainment form of brainwashing glues the audience to the TV every week or even everyday and begin to upload subliminal messages into their brains, making it hard to have a mind of their own. The writers of programs or music are the ones directing the way people should think, making them worshipers of human beings who are considered superstars like lady Gaga, Madonna, Justin Bieber, Beatles, Elvis Presley, Rolling Stones and a lost of others who are dead or alive. If you watch old footage of Beatles or Elvis, you will see many brainwashed women crying and even fainting because they saw these superstars.

How about the videos or computer games, including the ones in cell phones? Is there any message there? Of course, they are also ideal items of brainwashing. Imaging a game where you are the hero in a war, killing the enemies without mercy. As you do that you score same points. What is the message in the game? You can kill anyone you consider enemies even though you have no reason to kill them. The truth is: the agents of control are brainwashing people right from childhood up to adulthood through all the means of entertainment like music, movies, computer game and a host of others. Programming humanity has gone to the extent that anyone that opposes conformity in ideals and dealings is an enemy, even if he or she is a member of his family.

At this point, I would refer to John Todd, the highest Illuminati defector in relation to brainwashing through entertainment. He says Rock and Roll music is designed to cast a demonic spell on the listeners. In his presentation, "Witchcraft of Rock and Roll" in the multimedia section on Henry Makow's web site Todd said that the Illuminati started Jesus Rock to control the message.

Anyone reading Todd's lecture can see he was raised Satanist as he claimed, and had a profound understanding. Fritz Springmeier, who is also imprisoned, said Todd knew things that had taken him (Springmeier) years to gasp.

I dare say at this junction that so many of the predictions in Todd's messages to humanity before he was imprisoned in 1987 had come to pass although he may not be correct about the dates. Such messages that sounded too bizarre to be believed then include the 9-11 attack, war on terror, the suspension of US constitutional protections, the erection of a police state, the failure of congress, the media, the dumbing down and homosexualization of society, the sexualization of children, the explicate Satanism, depravity and pornography in the entertainment industries. Considering what is happening all around the world in light with these messages, John Todd makes a lot of sense.

Henry Makow puts it this way: "Humanity is the victim of a monstrous conspiracy of unspeakable proportions. Our leaders whom we pay to defend us from this sort of thing are either dupes or traitors."

The agents of control have really gone far in brainwashing leaders at various capacities, including political, religious and other leaders, using all means of communication, education, entertainment and information to reduce humanity into vegetables or robots that can be directed with a remote control. It started right from the time we were young when means of entertainment like music, movies, books and cartoons are used as weapons to manipulate and control our minds without anyone suspecting it.

Most of people all over the world are living in the dreams of these agents of control through all forms of entertainments. If we live there for too long, reality will become nightmare when we make up. It would be better to appreciate the truth right now before the lies of agents of control create havoc for humanity.

CHAPTER SEVEN

BRAINWASHING THROUGH RELIGION

According to David Nicholls, religious indoctrination is real. It is a traditionally based process of all cultures. All religions work on the principle of exposing each new generation to a single world view, to the exclusion of all others in a repetitions and authoritative manner. Doubts as to the veracity of such teachings are not encouraged, indeed are not tolerated. Once learned, the information so gained is retained for life, allowing it to take on an instinctive mantle in later years. As with all acquired knowledge, such as learning to ride a bicycle or remembrance of mathematical time's tables, once taught, unlearning is not an easy option. This is not to say that the results of such methodology are not practically overcome-able.

Youthful brains soak up information with little efforts, establishing permanent neuronic pathways. Older brains required considerably more effort to alter this situation. There are many Atheists to attest to this. In fact, it is the rule rather than the rarity that most Atheists were raised from infancy under some religious regime or other. Even the most intense religious indoctrination can be overcome.

David Nicholls' view about religious indoctrination is only one out of many other ways of brainwashing through religion.

Let us study the case of Steven Hassan who joined the Unification Church in the 1970s and was a member for more than two years. He now works as a counselor and has written books about cults and their techniques. Here is his story as he wrote it.

"I consider myself to be an independent thinker. I was an advanced honours student. I had skipped eighth grade. I cycled across US when I was 16. I did not think I was vulnerable to being brainwashed by a cult.

"I was 19, and it was the beginning of the spring semester at college when three women, dressed like students, asked if they could sit at my table in the cafeteria. They were kind of flirting with me. I thought I was going to get a date. At some point, they said they were

part of a student movement, trying to make the world a better place. I said, 'are you part of some sort of religious group?' They said no. They also didn't say they were celibate and that Reverend Moon was going to match people and tell them why they could have sex. If they had, I would have said, 'you're crazy, leave me alone.' I say this to highlight the point about deception: people don't knowingly join cults.

"Little did I know that, within a few weeks, I would be told to drop out of school, donate my bank account, look at Moon as my true parent, and believe my parents were Satan. I didn't even believe in Satan until I met the group.

"I hadn't heard of the Moonies and I didn't know about Moon himself until several weeks into my indoctrination. These new people picked me up on a Friday evening and drove me to a very expensive mansion, which turned out to be one of their headquarters. As we were driving through the gate, they said, 'by the way, we are having a joint workshop with the Unification Church!' I said nobody had told me about a workshop or a Church. They did the classic mind control technique - they turned it around and made it my issue. 'What's the matter?' they said. 'Are you closed-minded?'

"I was put in a dormitory and couldn't sleep. I was planning to get out of there the next day, but morning came and I was told I had missed the van. They said I would regret it for the rest of my life if I didn't stay, and talked me into a 40-day separation, where I shouldn't communicate with my friends and family.

"Each evening we had to write feedback. At the end of the last day I remember writing. I am too blown away to write anything now! My mind was exploding. At lectures, they had introduced the idea that all human history was culminating, that God was sending the messiah and that the third world war was going to happen in the next three years. What did I want to do? Did I want to be part of this great and glorious thing, or did I want to be selfish and go back to my little life?

"Within three months I was a cult leader. I got very deeply involved, and I got to the point where I was being told to think about what country I wanted to run when we took over the world.

"I was with the Moonies for two and a half years. I worked 21 hours a day, seven days a week - in prayer for between one and three hours. Then I would spend the rest of the day doing PR or lectures for

the group, recruiting and fund-raising. Everyone on my team was told they had to raise a minimum of $100.00 a day, other wise they wouldn't be allowed to sleep, and as a good leader, if they couldn't sleep, I couldn't either. I had gone three days without sleep when I crashed a van into the back of a tractor trailer.

"They gave me tapes of Moon's speeches to listen to in the hospital when I was recovering from the crash, but you can only do that for so many hours in the day. Out of the controlled environment, I really missed my younger sister. I called her and told her I had been in an accident. She told the rest of my family.

"They hired former members (of the Moonies) to do an intervention with me. It was very difficult experience because I was programmed to fear Satan and anyone who criticized Moon. I thought it was test of faith and I was convinced I hadn't been brainwashed.

"My father started to weep at one point and said: 'what would you do if it was your son who had dropped out of college, cut off contact?' I could feel he was genuinely concerned about me, but I didn't mean I wanted to leave. I neither think Moon was not the Messiah. He asked me to listen to them for the next five days, and at the end if I still wanted to go back he would take me there. I wanted to prove to them I wasn't brainwashed, but on the fifth day, as soon as I allowed the thought that Moon was a liar into my consciousness it was like a house of cards falling down. I was horrified.

"I didn't do anything for three months after the de-programming. I just tried to work out who I was and what I believed. After three months, I realized I wanted to go public and exposed it, which I have been doing ever since, writing books about these groups work and working as a therapist to protect people.

"Now Moon is gone (dead), I'm concerned that the cult will start generating stories about how he walked on water and raised dead people. My fear is that for the sake of the franchise they will come together and promote Moon as a great being."

There are few things to consider in Steven Hassan's ugly experiences of brainwashing through religion.

Firstly, it is instructive to note that the case of Unification Church is a very minor fraction of the arm of the agent of control through religion. Going by the various results of research works, the agent of control has mind bulging web of lies that are aimed at what is dubbed New World Order.

Secondly, a well packaged lie in the form of truth is very destructive to human mind, let alone chains of packages of lies. Besides that, lies that are hidden between truths are so powerful and destructive enough to wipe out a whole generation of truth.

We also have this area of magical or demonic powers to think of. How does it affect a person? Well, considering some supernatural events that often take place, one cannot help but to believe there are demonic powers. What is the source? Satan or Lucifer is believed to be behind it. If there is a belief in Satan, then we also have to consider the belief in God. Through that, we can balance the scale and understand what exactly in happening in the world.

CHAPTER EIGHT

THE BELIEF IN GOD IN QUESTION

There is an argument in a classroom between a Christian student and a professor of philosophy who is a diehard Atheist. Unlike in some arguments that are scripted by agents of mind control to sway the minds of audience to their side, this argument is based on science, information and sound opinions. The story goes like this.

The Professor of philosophy said to his students in the class, "let me explain the problem science has with Jesus Christ." The atheist professor paused before he looked at one of his new students. He told him to stand up. "You're a Christian, aren't you, son?"

"Yes, sir," the student replied. "Absolutely."

"Is God good?" the professor asked.

"Sure! God is good, and I will keep the faith."

"Is God all powerful? Can God do anything?"

"Yes."

"Are you good or evil?"

"The Bible says I'm evil."

The professor grinned knowingly. "Aha! The Bible!" He thought for a moment. "Here is one for you. Let's say there's a sick person over there and you can cure him. You can do it. Would you help him? Would you try?"

"Yes, sir, I would," the student replied.

"So you're good...!"

"I wouldn't say that."

"But why not say that? You'll help a sick and maimed person if you could. Most of us would if we could. But God doesn't."

The student did not answer. So the professor continued, "God doesn't, does he? My brother was a Christian who died of cancer, even though he prayed to Jesus to heal him. How is this Jesus good? Hmmm? Can you answer that one?"

The student remained silent.

"No, you can't, can you?" the professor asked. He took a sip of water from a glass on his desk to give the student time to relax. "let's

start again, young fella. Is God good?"

"Er... Yes, "the student says.

"Is Satan good?"

The student did not hesitate to answer, "no"

"Then where does Satan comes from?"

The student faltered, "from.... God..."

"That's right," the professor said gleefully." God made Satan, didn't he? Tell me, son. Is there evil in this world?"

"Yes, sir."

"Evil is everywhere, isn't it? And God did make everything, correct?"

"Yes, sir."

"So who created evil?"

Again, the student has no answer.

"Is there sickness? Immorality? Hatred? Ugliness? All these terrible things. Do they exist in this world?"

The student squirmed on his feet, "yes."

"So who created them?"

The student did not answer again. So the professor repeated his question, "who created them?"

There is still no answer. Suddenly the lecturer broke away to pace in front of the classroom. The class was mesmerized. "Tell me," he continued, apparently enjoying himself. "Do you believe in Jesus Christ, son?"

The student's voice betrayed him and cracked, "yes, professor, I do."

The professor stopped pacing. "Science says you five senses, you use to identify and observe the world round you. Have you ever seen Jesus?"

"No, sir, I've never seen Him."

"Then tell us if you've ever heard your Jesus?"

"Perhaps not, sir."

"Have you ever felt your Jesus, tasted your Jesus or smelt your Jesus? Have you ever had any sensory perception of Jesus Christ or God for that matter?"

"Perhaps not."

"Yet you still believe in him?"

"Yes."

"According to the rules of empirical, testable, demonstrable protocol, science says your God doesn't exist. What do you say to that, son?"

"Nothing," the student replied. "I only have my faith."

"Yes, faith," the professor repeated. "And that is the problem science has with God. There is no evidence, only faith."

The student stood quietly for a moment before asking a question of his own. "Professor, is there such thing as heat?"

"Yes," the professor replied. "There is heat."

"And is there such a thing as cold?"

"Yes, son. There is cold too."

"No, sir, there isn't."

The professor turned to face the student. He was obviously interested. The room suddenly became very quiet. The student began to explain. "You can have lots of heat, even more heat, super heat, mega-heat, white heat, a little heat or no heat, but we don't have anything called a cold. We can hit 458 degrees below zero, which is no heat, but you can't go any further after that. There is no such thing as cold; otherwise we would be able to go colder than 458 degrees. You see, sir, cold is only a word we used to describe the absence of heat. We cannot measure cold but we can measure heat in thermal units because heat is energy. Cold is not the opposite of heat, sir, just the absence of it."

There was complete silence across the room. A pen drops somewhere in the classroom, sounding like a hammer.

"What about darkness, professor? Is there such a thing as darkness?"

"Yes," the professor replied without hesitation. "What is night if it isn't darkness?"

"You're wrong again, sir. Darkness is not something. It is absence of something. You can have low light, normal light, bright light, flashing light... but if you have no light constantly you have nothing and it's called darkness, isn't it? That's the meaning we use to define the word. In reality, darkness doesn't exist. If it does, you would be able to make darkness darker, wouldn't you?"

The professor began to smile at the student. He thought this would be a good semester.

He asked, "so what point are you making, young man?"

"Yes, professor. My point is, your philosophical premise is flawed to start with and so your conclusion must be flawed."

The professor could not hide his surprise this time.

"Flawed? Can you explain how?"

"You are working on the premise of duality." the student explained. "You argue that there is life and there's death, a good God and a bad God. You are viewing the concept of God as something we can measure. Sir, science can't even explain a thought. It uses electricity and magnetism, but has never seen, much less fully understood either one. To view death as opposite of life is to be ignorant of the fact that death cannot exists as a substantive thing. Death is not the opposite of life, just the absence of it. Now tell me, professor. Do you teach your students that they evolved from a monkey?"

"If you are referring to the natural evolutionary process, young man, yes, of course, I do."

"Have you ever observed evolution with your own eyes, sir?"

The professor began to shake his head, still smiling, as he realized the trend of the argument - a very good semester indeed.

"Since no one has ever observed the process of evolution at work and cannot even prove that this process is an on-going endeavor, are you not teaching your own opinion, sir? Are you not now a scientist, but a preacher?"

The class went gaga with uproar. The student remained silent until the commotion subsided.

"To continue the point you were making earlier, let me give you an example of what I mean?" the student said, looking around the room. "Is there anyone in the class who has ever seen the professor's brain?"

The class burst into laughter.

"Is there anyone here who has ever heard the professor's brain, felt the professor's brain, touched or smelt the professor's brain? No one appeared to have done so. So, according to the established rules of empirical, testable, demonstrable protocol, science says that you have no brain, with all due respect, sir. So if science says you have no brain, how can we trust your lectures, sir?"

Now the room was dead silent. The professor just stared at the student, his face unreadable.

Finally, after what seemed an eternity, the professor answered, "I guess you'll have to take them to faith."

That ended the argument. The class knew who won.

No doubt, Christianity has a lot of influence in this world. For more than two thousand years since the death of Jesus Christ, the influence of the religion cannot be quantified. It is so dominant that the time of birth and death of Jesus Christ is used as form of dating period. When you hear dates like 10BC, 20BC, it actually implies Before Christ. When you hear 10AD, 20AD, it implies After Death of Christ. In fact, the year we are in now which is 2015 means two thousand and fifteen years After Death of Christ. Some skeptics like the Atheists argue that Christ never exist as we see it in the argument but the date proves them wrong. If Christ exists, why is it so important to man that his birth and death are used to come up with dating periods? Why didn't the world use the period of birth and death of great people or kings like Alexander, the great, Caesar and a host of others to come up with dating period? This question actually calls for exploration of Christianity through the Christian Bible. So we need to see what the Bible have got to say to so many questions in the next chapter.

CHAPTER NINE

<u>THE BIBLE AT A GLANCE</u>

Since the basis of Christianity in question is found in the Bible, we need to have a glace at it and consider a few things about God, the people, the world and possibly the devil if we can tolerate the information inside it.

According to Wikipedia, many fields of study compare the Bible and history, ranging from archeology and astronomy to linguistics and comparative literature. Studying the Bible may provide insight into ancient and modern culture, mythology and morality. Scholars also examine the historical context of Bible passages, the importance ascribed to events by the authors, and the contrast between the descriptions of these events and historical evidence.

One of these evidences is perhaps what is known as the Dead Sea Scrolls. The material is papyrus, parchment, and Bronze writing in Hebrew, Aramaic, Greek and Nabataean. It was created around 408 BC to 318 AD.

The Dead sea scrolls are a collection of 972 texts discovered between 1946 and 1956 at Khirbe Qumran in the West Bank. They were found in caves about a mile inland from the northwest shore of the Dead Sea, from which they derive their name.

The texts are of great historical, religious and linguistic significance because they include the earliest known surviving manuscript of the works later included in the Hebrew Bible canon.

Having given the brief historical value of the Bible, let us consider a few things about it.

According to the New International Version (NIV) of the Bible, published by Biblica, Inc, in Colorado, United States, the Bible is a collection of letters, poems, stories, visions, prophetic oracles, wisdom and other kinds of writings. The version also describes the Bible story as a drama that has to be acted out, performed and lived. It is an activated story that is performed on the stage by everybody everyday with no one excepted. One of the keys to engaging the Bible well is to recognize that the story has not ended.

God's saving action still continues. In other words, the Bible distinguishes Christianity from any form of religion and proclaim it as a way of life as designed by God.

Here goes the life as designed by God in the form series of Acts or Scenarios.

Act 1: It begins with God on stage, creating the world. He makes a man and a woman called Adam and Eve, placing them in Garden of Eden to work and taken care of it. The earth is created to be their home. His intention is for humanity to be close to Him. Human beings are God's image bearers, created to share in the task of bringing God's wise and beneficial rule to the rest of the world. This Act also reveals that life is a gift from the Creator, telling us what human beings are made for, and providing the setting for all the actions that follows.

Act 2: Tension and conflict are introduced into the story when Adam and Eve decided to go their own way and seek their own wisdom. They listen to the deceptive voice of God's enemy, Satan and doubt God's trustworthiness. They decide to live apart from the word that God himself has given them.

The disobedience of Adam and Eve introduces sins into the world with devastating consequences. Heaven and earth - God's realm and realm of human beings were intended to be united but now God is hidden. Now it is possible to be in the world without knowing God, without experiencing his presence, without following His ways and without living in gratitude.

As a result of this rebellion, the first exile in the story takes place. The humans are driven away from God's presence. Their offsprings through out history will seek to find their way back to the source of life. They will devise any number of philosophies and religions, trying to make sense out of a fallen, yet haunting world. But death now stalks them. They realize that they cannot escape it.

New questions arise in the drama: Can the curse on creation be overcome and the relationship between God and humanity restored? Can heaven and earth be reunited? Or has God's enemy effectively ended the plan and subverted the story?

ACT3: Still following his direction of redemptive plan, God calls Abraham and promises to make him into a great nation. God narrows his focus and concentrates on one group of people but his ultimate goal remains the same: to bless all the people on earth and remove the curse from creation. When Abraham's descendants are enslaved in Egypt, a central pattern in the story is set: God hears their cries for help and comes to set them free. God makes a covenant with this new nation of Israel at Mount Sinai. Israel is called by God to be a light to the nations, showing the world what it means to follow God's ways for living. God, however, warns them that if they are not faithful to the covenant, he will send them away just as he did with Adam and Eve. In spite of God's repeated warnings through his prophets, Israel seems determined to break the covenant. So God abandons the holy temple - the sign of his presence with his people - and it is smashed by pagan invaders. Israel's capital city Jerusalem is sacked and burned.

Abraham's descendants, chosen to reverse the failure of Adam, have now apparently also failed. God, however, remains committed to his people and his plan, so he sows the seed of a different outcome. He promises to send a new king, a descendant of Israel's great king David, who will lead the nation back to its destiny. The very prophets who warned Israel of the dire consequences of its wrong doing also pledges that the good news of God's victory will be heard in Israel once again.

Act 4: ends tragically with God apparently absent and the pagan nations ruling over Israel but the hope of a promise remains. God will send his anointed one - the messiah.

Act 5: "He is the god made manifest... the universal Saviour of human life." These words referring to Caesar Augustus (found in a Roman inscription from 4BC in Ephesus) proclaims the gospel of the Roman Empire. This version of good news announces that Caesar is the lord who brings peace, and prosperity to the world. Into this empire, a son of David is born, and he announces the gospel of God's kingdom. Jesus of Nazareth "brings the goal news of the coming of God's reign". He begins to show what God's new creation looks like. He announces the end of Israel's exile and the

35

forgiveness of sins. He heals the sick and raises the dead. He overcomes the dark spiritual powers. He welcomes sinners and those who are considered unclean. Jesus renews the nation, rebuilding the twelve tribes of Israel around himself in a symbolic way. But the established religions leaders are threatened by Jesus and his kingdom, so they have him brought before the Roman governor. During the very week the Jews were remembering and celebrating Passover - God's ancient rescue of his people from slavery in Egypt - the Romans nail Jesus to a cross and kill him as a false king. But the Bible indicates that this defeat is actually God's greatest victory. How? Jesus willingly gives up his life as a sacrifice on behalf of the nation, on behalf of the world. Jesus takes onto himself the full force of evil and empties it of its power. In this surprising way, Jesus fights and wins Israel's ultimate battle. The real enemy was never Rome, but the spiritual powers that lie behind Rome and every other kingdom whose weapon is death. Through his blood, Jesus pays the price and reconciles everything in heaven and on earth to God.

God then publicly declares this victory by reversing Jesus death sentence and raising him back to life. The resurrection is the great sign that the new creation has begun. Jesus is the fulfillment of Israel's story and a new start for the entire human race. Death came through the first man, Adam. The resurrection of the dead through the new man, Jesus, God's original intention is being reclaimed.

ACT 6: If the key victory has already been secured, why is there an ACT 6? They answer is that God wants the victory of Jesus to spread to all nations of the world. The risen Jesus says to his disciples, "peace be with you! As the father has sent me, I am sending you." So this new act in the drama tells the story of how the earliest followers of Jesus began to spread the good news of God's reign. According to the New Testament, all those who belong to Israel's messiah are children of Abraham, heirs of both the ancient promises and the ancient mission. The task of bringing blessing to the peoples of the world has been given again to Abraham's family. Their mission is to live out the liberating message of the good news of God's kingdom. God is gathering people from all around the world and forming them into assemblies of Jesus' followers - his Church. Together they are God's new temple, the place where his Spirit lives. Forgiveness of sins and reconciliation with God can now be announced to all.

CHAPTER TEN

THE FINAL ACT IN THE BIBLE

In Act 6, according to the New International Version of the Bible in the activated story of God and humanity, the Bible is made to appear like the story of the central struggle, wearing its way through history of the world. And now the story arrives at its own time, involving everybody in its drama. So the challenge of a decision confronts us. What will we do? How are we going to fit into this story? What role are we going to play? God is inviting us to be a part of his mission of recreation - of bringing restoration, justice and forgiveness. We are to join in the task of making things new, to be a living sign of what is to come when the drama is complete.

FINAL ACT: God's future has come into our world through the work of Jesus, the Messiah. But for now, the present evil age also continues. Brokenness, wrong doing, sickness and even death remain. We live in the time of the overlap of the ages, the time of in-between. The final Act is coming, but it has not arrived. We live in the time of invitation, when the call of the gospel goes out to every creature. Of course, many still live as though God does not exist. They do not acknowledge the rule of the messiah. But the day is coming when Jesus will return to earth and the reign of God will become uncontested reality throughout the world.

God's presence will be fully and openly with us once again, as, it was at the beginning of the drama. God's plan of redemption will reach its goal. The creation will experience its own Exodus, finding freedom from its bondage to decay. Pain and tears, regret and shame, suffering and death will be no more.

When the day of resurrection arrives, God's people will find that their hope has been realized. The dynamic force of an indestructible life will course through their bodies. Empowered by the Spirit, and unhindered by sin and death, we will pursue our original vocation as a renewed humanity. We will be culture makers, under God but over the world. Having been remade in the image of Christ, we will share in bringing his wise, caring rule of the earth. At the centre of it all will be God himself. He will return and make his home with us, this time in a new heavens and a new earth.

This story is about the summary of the Bible of the Christians. If you ask of my opinion at this stage, I would say it is a very wonderful story. I have read the whole Bible two or three times for knowledge about God and for research work like this book. Actually, it is not my opinion that counts right now but the truth.

Anatole France says, "if 50 million people say a foolish thing, it is still a foolish thing." And I dare add this to his quote, "if 50 million people believe a lie, it is still a lie." Again, according to George Orwell, in a time of universal deceit - telling the truth is a revolutionary act.

I want to use the story of a woman called Debra Pursell as a case study to prove whether the story of the Bible is real or not. If the drama in the Bible is not real, no one has anything to be worried about. If it is real, however, humanity is doomed unless everybody turns to the God of the Christians.

The story is titled: I knocked At Hell's Gate. Here it goes as Debra wrote it:

'I grew up in a house - not a home. You may grow up in a "house" too - something like mine. A house is where four walls surround you. Inside those four walls is constant conflict and hurt. There is no hugging.... very few kind words. A home has kind, gentle, warm words of love... a hug now and then .... laughter... security... warmth in relationships. I wish I would have a home like that to grow up in, but it wasn't to be. Nevertheless, I am thankful that I at least have a house to grow up in. Some hardly even have that.

'Through high school, I was "blessed" with a counselor who essentially convinced me that I would never amount to much. Have others somehow made me feel like I am slow and dumb?

'When I was in the 11th grade of school, my fragile world became even more shattered. My father had been in the hospital for some time. He had cirrhosis of the liver due to alcohol abuse, though I didn't know it until later on in life. Every day after high school, I would go to the hospital and visit him. I loved him so much. I asked Jesus over and over not to let my father go away. He looked so terrible. But I believed Jesus would make him better. At certain times he would

say to me, "Debra, I love you. I'm truly sorry. I'm really sorry. Please, forgive me." I really didn't know what to forgive him for.

"My grandmother (whom I also loved very much) painted china, and she helped me paint a plate with a horse on it for my father. I took it to him and he was greatly pleased with the gift, but he didn't want it kept there at the hospital. He told me to take it home, and he would be coming home soon as well. I believed him.

'The next day at school they called me to the office. The counselor that I admired so "greatly" broke the news to me about as cold as she could possibly have delivered it: "your father is dead."

'I refused to believe her. I was convinced she was lying to torment me. "I just saw him yesterday! He said not dead!" I was almost delirious and near shock.

' "No- he's dead," came her cold retort. "Accept it."

'I fell over on the floor. The pain was just to much for me to bear. All I could do was ask, "why Jesus, why? I loved my dad so much. Why? Everything I love goes away."

'After that... I began to think to myself that maybe I shouldn't love.

'Years passed, and I managed to graduate from high school and then started attending college. I had a vacuum inside me though. I wanted someone to love, and someone who would love me. I was vulnerable classic - I was attracted to men who abused me. All I had known was abuse growing up, and I didn't feel I deserved any better as I grew older.

'I became pregnant and was counseled to have an abortion. I knew it was wrong, but the pressure to go through with it was more than I could stand up to. I was taken to an abortion clinic by my soon to be husband in Detroit, Michigan. There were a number of women there, waiting to have abortions as well, and they acted as if it's an everyday thing... I felt so alone and so afraid... I did not want to kill my baby inside me; I was so confused in my head. I didn't know what I should do. When it was my turn the nurse took me to a changing room. I changed into a gown. As I stood there, my head was racing. I pecked down the hall, snuck out and tried to run away. One of the nurses caught me and took me back, saying, "I don't think you should do this. You see, the money was already paid." I think I remember asking Jesus to forgive me. I know I did later and I always for a lot of

years, until someone told me you only need to ask once. Jesus forgets and the sin is no more.

'I married the guy who got me pregnant. I didn't have anyone else to turn to, even though I didn't love him. He went into the Air Force. I became a military wife. We went off to Texas and lived there for six weeks. His neglect and abuse of me grew worse. He got an assignment in Greece, and we spent two years there. He was a military police man. He grew more hardened, at least around me. There was more physical abuse along with the verbal abuse.

'When his two-year tow was finished in Greece, he got reassigned to the United States again. I got pregnant with my first child. I had a little girl, named Rachael. She was so special. Then a boy came along. We named him Philip. By the time Philip came along, the pain in the marriage was nearly at the bursting point. My husband had an affair, but because I simply refused to believe divorce was an option, I stayed with him. Then he had another affair and this time he wanted a divorce from me. I refused, but he filed for one anyway and it went through. He left me and our two children for a while, but then came back with what appeared to be some compassionated concern, and suggested he take the two children for a month so I could have a rest. I thought it was a good idea, but the moment I stepped off that military base he got papers filed that I had abandoned my children. They were taken away from me...."

Well, this is not the end of the story or the real life drama so to say but at this point, I have to indicate that this is a battle between life and death, light and darkness sanity and insanity, right and wrong, good and bad, positive and negative, heaven and hell. Debra is going through her own battle just like every other people. When the story is concluded, we will discuss this battle.

CHAPTER ELEVEN

THE WORLD BATTLES

With the study case of Debra Pursell, we can see from what she has gone through so far that she was going through a battle which she could not possibly comprehend. The mere fact that she did not realized who the real enemy was is more than enough to lose the battle she is facing. If you think her real enemy is her counselor who made her believed she would not amount to anything, you are missing the point. If you think it is her parents who never build her a home that is filled with love, you're wrong. If you think it is her husband who abused and later dumped her, taking away her children who meant the whole world to her, again you are wrong. In the concluding part of the story, you would see who the real enemy is. Then we can talk about him. After all, there is no way you can be engaged in battle without at least an enemy. So let's go back to Debra Pursell's story: "I knocked At Hell's Gate."

'... When the children were taken away from me, like so many times before... I asked, "why, Jesus? Why? What have I done so bad to be treated this wrong?" Then in the confusion and hurt, I began to grow bitter at Jesus. I know it was wrong, but I just couldn't help it.

'I met some girls and entered the party scene. I didn't care about my life. My friend and I partied almost every night, and all weekend I drank a lot because I didn't care. No matter how much I sinned against God, the next day when I sobered up, I would ask Jesus to forgive me. I would tell him I was sorry for acting the terrible way I had acted the night before, and that I loved him. I would ask for his help because I would feel like a piece of a puzzle that didn't belong anywhere.

'I took a barmaid job and began to grow hard. I swore and didn't care. I hurt people and didn't care. I used men and found pleasure in it - I felt power in it.

'I had been going with friends to a palm reader. This palm reader kept telling me things that are going to happen in my life, and I would believe her. I didn't care about the warnings the Bible gives about

doing such things. I was blinded to the fact that this is a gate way to the demonic realm.

'I was really tired one night after working and went to bed early. Around 3 am in the morning, I woke up sharply with hot sweat. Two figures stood at the foot of my bed. I rubbed my eyes, saying to myself, "who is it? Who is there?"

'One figure was all dressed in black with a hood over its head. The other figure was all dressed in white. They were standing quite far apart. The figure in black kept shaking its head back and forth. The figure in white was waving to me, smiling. I kept rubbing my eyes because I wasn't really certain this was actually happening, or I was having some kind of delusion. Then in an instant they both disappeared. I dismissed the whole thing a few days later, though it left me with a very eerie feeling.

'I kept living the same rebellious lifestyle after that. I didn't heed the warning. The girl I partied a lot with for some reasons went to her house earlier than usual one night. I went to her house about half an hour later. We left and went to Dunkins Donuts. My friend had a bottle of rum in the car and we both were drinking rum and coke, our usual things. I didn't want a lot of rum in my cup because I was driving that night.

'I remember putting on my seatbelt and we pulled out of the parking lot of Dunkin Donuts and drove on down the highway. At the first stoplight, it turned red and I stopped. We were listening to music, and when the light turned green, I started moving forward. Then out of nowhere, a car was coming at us at high speed, running the light. I remember my friend yelling, "Oh my God!" - just before the car hit us.

'I left my body. I started going down this long, dark tunnel. It was dark.... so dark. I knew I was dead and I was going to hell. I was yelling, "I don't want to go yet! I don't want to go yet!" I'm falling further and farther away from the little light at the top of the tunnel above me. Out of the dark, things began grabbing at me. Long fingernails began to grab and claw at me, trying to pull me into them. I kept screaming, "No! I don't want to go yet!"

'Their hideous mouths were opened wide and their teeth were gnashing at me. Then I began pleading with Jesus, "Jesus, no... don't let me go to hell! I'll do right! Please, give me another chance. I'll do *right!" I begged and pleaded with him.*

'Suddenly my body stopped and there was a flash of light. It was like I was suspended in mid-air. Then I felt the impression of hands on my bottom, and the hands pushed me so fast... I saw myself going back towards the light at the top of the tunnel.

'The next thing I remember is that I woke up in the hospital. At first my eyes were closed, and when I opened them up, looking around to see where I was, I was confused. In my confusion, I heard a policeman say, "Oh - we lost this one. Do you have her name - anything on her?"

'I opened my eyes wider and said, "No, you didn't lose me!" He jumped back, scared out of his wits. The nurses and doctors came running in and the place was mass pandemonium. There is blood coming from me everywhere. They're pulling glass out of my body - there was a big piece above my eye. All I could do was lay there and sob... thanking Jesus for saving me from that dark pit I was in - being taken to hell...'

After the accident, Debra Pursell never remained the same again. She became a committed Christian.

At this point again, I must declare that I am a Christian. In fact I am a Pastor of a local Church in Nigeria. So I am going to use the last few chapters in this book to explain things that seem so mysterious to human minds. My references will be taken from the New king James study Bible, published by Thomas Nelson, Inc. I hope you are still with me up to this point. These last few chapters are so vital that without them, the conflicts within human mind cannot be resolved, the insanity cannot be cured, the confusion cannot be removed and the truth cannot be completely established.

The first thing I want you to note which Debra Pursell failed to realize then is that there is an enemy of mankind. Despite seeing her enemy physically in her room and her Saviour, Jesus, at the same time, she still could not resolve the conflict within her. So many people must have gone through the same experience and yet failed to identify the real enemy. Why is this so? The reason is simple. Everybody had been brainwashed at one point on the other, going by the results of this research work. If you have not been brainwashed by brainwashed parents, you would have been brainwashed by brainwashed teachers in the school. If you have not been brainwashed in the school, the chances are that you would have been brainwashed by publications, including books written by brainwashed authors. If by any chance, you have not been brainwashed by these, you would have been brainwashed by media or entertainment industries through the use of movies, music, cartoons and computer games that are created by agents of control. The question is: who is behind the washing of our brains? What exactly does he want to achieve through that? I believe the talk about the enemy of mankind will provide answers.

Now let us consider the passage in the Gospel according to Saint John chapter 10 verse 10. Jesus said in that passage, "The thief does not come except to steal, and to kill, and to destroy. I have come that they (the people) may have life, and that they may have it more abundantly." Just as the New International Version of the Bible has rightly compared the story in the Bible as a life drama and life-long scenarios which involve everybody playing his or her roles, the two figures that revealed themselves to Debra Pursell are the invisible key players or directors in the drama of real life.

The thief called the devil, according to what Jesus said, steals the soul of man while he (Jesus) redeems it. The thief brings about spiritual and eternal death while Jesus brings life to those who are spiritually dead. The thief brings about total destruction of souls in hell while, as we see it Debra's case, Jesus brings total restoration. The thief is the cause of darkness in her life while Jesus gives her light. Because she was blindfolded or brainwashed by the things or situation around her, she opted for darkness. She actually belongs to Jesus, going by her constant confession of him but she was stolen from him by the dark figure. When her choices began to take her to a place of eternal destruction after the accident that clearly claimed her life, Jesus who is represented by the light gave her the second chance. This is a great privilege because it is not everybody that gets the second chance to come back to life after death.

I had similar experience that makes me appreciate and understand the testimony of Debra Pursell better. There are several other people like Angelica Zambrano, former Atheist Professor Howard Storm and a whole lot of others who had similar experiences.

The determination of the thief to steal the gift of freewill that is given to man by God is evident through out all generations. The struggle of man to keep his freewill becomes an aged-long battle that began right from the time Adam and Eve were driven away from the Garden of Eden. This obscure battle is what actually makes our world a battlefield which most people are not conscious of. We have an enemy who has stolen our kingdom, planning to steal the souls of men and then take them to hell. These are the simple explanations about the enemy of mankind and his deadly missions in this world.

CHAPTER TWELVE

HOW THE BATTLE BEGAN

You might have heard different versions of how the universe came into being. Some may be true, some may be partly true and some may be entirely false. Nobody can afford to miss the whole truth, based on the Bible. Going through the Bible over times for the purpose of this kind of teaching, I discover the truth and narrate the story about the formation of what I call three kingdoms in one of my books titled: The Redeemer And The Dragon. This is a Bible based truth and nothing more to it. I must warn you, however, that the truth may cause a riot in your intellect because, as George Orwell had been quoted, "humanity is used to a web of lies, making truth a revolutionary thing to accept." Still, man needs freedom from this web of lies and Jesus said in Gospel according to Saint John chapter 8 verse 32, "And you shall know the truth, and the truth shall make you free."

The summary of story about The Redeemer And The Dragon goes thus:

There is a kingdom called Eternity. It has no beginning and no end. The name of the king is called The Father. He has subjects who are Eternal Beings that worship and praise Him day in day out. The praise leader is called Lucifer, the son of morning, according to the book of Isaiah chapter 14 verse 12.

Lucifer was doing a good job in leading others to praise The Father until, according to verse 13 of the same chapter and book, he decided to establish his own throne in Eternity.

The implication of that was to make himself the king in the kingdom of The Father. War broke out in Eternity, according to Revelation chapter 12 verse 7. Lucifer who is later called by many names with his co-rebels who are later called demons or devils engaged warriors in Eternity under the leadership of the arch angel called Michael in the battle for superiority. Michael and the warriors fought and defeated Lucifer and the demons. They were thrown out of Eternity and made to wander on the face of the earth that was then void, full of darkness and without form, according to

47

the book of Genesis chapter 1 verses 1 to the end. The earth was later recreated by The Father and handed over to the first couple called Adam and Eve. Although it is not quite clear at which point another kingdom called hell was created for demons and Lucifer but it can assumed that it is shortly after the rebels were thrown out of Eternity. According to the book of Revelation chapter 21 verse 8, hell is made up of fire and brimstone. It was actually created for Lucifer and the demons, not for man.

When The Father created the earth, he gave it to Adam and Eve to rule. They have the power to stop Lucifer and the demons from invading their kingdom. They also have the authority to rule other creatures, going by Genesis chapter 1 verse 28. In the same book in chapter 2 verse 16, at the same time, The Father gave the couple the law of dominion. Breaking this law meant losing the kingdom and even their lives and access to kingdom of Eternity called heaven. According to the book of Revelation, chapter 12 verse 9, the devil or Satan or Lucifer transformed himself into a serpent who deceives the whole world. He went to influence Adam and Eve to break the law of dominion that was given to them by The Father, according to Genesis chapter 3 verses 1 to 7. In the rest of the verses of the chapter, we see how man lost his kingdom to Satan when he was driven out of the palace called Garden of Eden, from where the couple was supposed to be ruling. The palace, so to say, was relocated to Paradise in Eternity by The Father. Ever since then, man and woman alike become slaves in the kingdom they were supposed to be king and queen - a very sorrowful drama indeed but, as International Version of the Bible says, the story is not completed yet.

Everybody in the world is playing a role whether consciously or unconsciously.

The battle that began in Eternity continued in the kingdom of man. It is a battle between what the Bible calls Eternal life and Eternal Death. It is a battle between man and his enemies - Lucifer and demons. It is a battle between Salvation (freedom) and Bondage (slavery). What made man a small god lies in the fact that the Almighty God called The Father gives him the power of will and choice. The power to chose between God and Satan who always poses as a friendly neighbour like the serpent, the power to chose between light and darkness, the power to chose between good and bad becomes too much for man to control. So Satan helps him to make wrong choices until God decides that the person that chose the wrong path shall end up in the place that is created for Lucifer and the demons in the lake of fire and brimstone, according to the book of Revelation chapter 21 verse 8.

Despite this declaration, man continues to make wrong choices because Satan continues to direct or influence him to think the wrong way through the use of his eyes, ears and other human senses. Because man is blind to the things of Eternity, he lives by sight instead of faith in God. Despite all the proofs of the works of God which man enjoys and despite the havoc Satan is doing to mankind through demonic rituals and human sacrifices, man still see him as a friend or the god they can trust. Some do not even believe there is God or devil as in case of the atheist professor. Indeed, the entire human race is going blind and insane.

God knows that man cannot save himself from Satan and the demons who keep the people perpetually in bondage. He, therefore, sent a messiah in the person of Jesus Christ, God the son, into the world. In Gospel according to Saint John chapter 3:16, the Bible says, "For God so loved the world that He gave His only begotten Son, that whosoever believes in Him should not perish but have everlasting life." Then real stage for the battle is reset by Lucifer through the use of human philosophies, religions, academics, entertainments and other forms of brainwashing. This often times brings about the argument about the deity of Jesus Christ like the case study of the atheist professor and his students. Another case study that typically expresses the misconceptions of people about the deity of Jesus Christ is that of an editor of religion column of a newspaper. He said, "to know God's will on current issues, we should try to get into the mind of Jesus." He suggested that we should set aside our differences in beliefs about deity of Jesus Christ, his atonement, and resurrection and think of him as a kind and good man instead. This idea sounds appealing but it is a way of perverting the truth. This kind of idea helps people make the mistakes that bring about different kinds of religions. Do not forget: Christianity is not a religion. It is a way of life as God designed it in real life drama that was explained in line with the

International Version of the Bible.

The passage that established the truth about Jesus is found in the Gospel according to Saint John chapter 1verses 1 to 5 which reads, "In the beginning was the Word and the Word was with God, and the Word was God. He was in the beginning with God.

"All things were made through Him, and without Him nothing was made. In Him was life, and the life was the light of men. And the light shines in the darkness, and the darkness did not comprehend it."

According to that passage, the world was created by the Word called Jesus and to prove that the world was created by Jesus, I would remind you that the Word inside God came out to recreate the world as we see it through out chapter 1 in the book of Genesis.

This word of God that created the world is what the Gospel, according to John, chapter 1 verses 1 to 5 is talking about. The purpose of this explanation would be defeated if you still consider Jesus less than God, The Son of The Father in Eternity. Disbelieving this truth can also lead to heresies, the parents of various forms of religions and cultism, including so many Christian cults like the Crusaders, Knight Malter, Moon, Jehovah witness, worship of virgin Mary, Mommon, New Age and a host of countless others.

Jesus established the fact in Gospel, according to Saint John chapter 14 verse 6 by saying, "I am the way, the truth and the life. No one comes to the Father except through me."

No one else in the history of man has ever made a claim like that without being proved wrong. This fact was established more than two thousand years ago and up till now, it is accepted as the truth because it is the truth.

A very fanatically religious man once questioned the deity of Jesus Christ few years ago by asking himself, "Who is this Jesus? Why is He so popular?" Then he had a dream about two men, each was standing at each path. The one on the right was standing smiling, waving at him to come to him because he is the way. The religious man looked at the other path and saw the founder of his religion, lying dead on the way. He wondered at the person he should ask about the right way to go. He went to the living man and asked, "where do I go, sir?" To which the man replied, "follow me. I am the way." Then he woke up, wondering at the dream. Coincidentally, so to say, he got a Bible and read the passage where Jesus says he is the way.

Jesus is much more than what man thinks He is because human minds are preoccupied by what they can see, hear, feel or perceive with their human senses as explained in the case study of the atheist professor. Unless man refuses to be moved by what he can perceive and allowed himself to be moved by the word of God in the Bible, building simple faith in Jesus, he cannot operate above the physical. The argument in the case study of the atheist professor proves that people has no other way of reaching out to God except through simple faith in Jesus Christ. This simple faith may appear childish if not foolish.

There is a case of one preacher leaving the hall where he just finished preaching. As he was outside, holding his Bible, one man approached him and said, "I admire your conviction and your sincerity when you preached in the hall but I have to tell you that the whole gospel is pure nonsense."

The preacher opened his Bible and said, "you're very right, you know. The word of God says exactly what you just said now."

"You're joking, right?" the man asked. "The Bible can't possibly say that the gospel is nonsense."

The preacher opened to 1 Corinthians 1:18 and read the place to him, "For the message of the cross is foolishness to those who are perishing, but to us who are saved it is the power of God."

The preacher closed his Bible and began to leave after establishing his point.

The man recognized it at once that the word of God sounded foolish to him because he was about to perish. He got hold of the preacher and requested him to tell him more. He became born again that day and then, from there, the word of God became the power of God to him.

The Bible says further in 1corinthians 1:21, "For since, in the wisdom of God, the world through wisdom did not know God, it pleased God through the foolishness of the message preached to save those who believe."

How does all explanations about the word of God sounds to you? Foolishness or power of God? It is not what you say alone that provides the answer but what you do. If you believe the word of God, you will follow it. By not following it, you make it appear like foolishness to you.

Why not go in your kneels right now, close your eyes and make this simple and brief prayer with your hearth? "Dear Lord, I just realized I have missed the way. Out of sheer ignorance, I have sinned against you, please, forgive me all my sins and let your Holy Spirit come into my life in Jesus name I pray. Amen.

If you just said that prayer, the implication of that is that you just become a child of God, going by the Gospel of Saint John chapter 1 verse 12. As a child of God, you now have powers and the right to operate as a child of God. This power, however, can be taken or reduced to nothing if you continue in sins and if you are not obedient to the word of God in the Bible, which you must read all the time. I would recommend to you The New King James, published by Thomas Nelson Publishers.

With your power as a child of God and the authority of the word of God, you can fight and defeat the enemy of mankind - Satan and his messengers.

CHAPTER THIRTEEN

THE POWER OF SURVIVAL

At this point I must declare that the insanity of humanity is actually characterized by he battles over the soul of man. The power to survive in this battle lies in our faith in Jesus Christ, the hope and the joy of the whole world.

To fully understand and appreciate the power of survival better, I wish to recommend to you my epic novel titled "The Battle Of The Conquerors" which treats the issue of battles of life in details.

Before I briefly shed light on the power of survival, it is instructive to note that everybody is involved in the battle of life just as we are all involved in the real life drama.

With the word of God in the Bible, I have established the fact that the war began in heaven - The Kingdom of Eternity that has no beginning and no end like engagement ring. The battle was brought down into the kingdom of man with Satan turning it against everybody in the world. Out of love of The Father, according to Gospel of Saint John chapter 3 verse 16, He sent Jesus Christ into the world, saying that whoever believes in Him would not perish in the war but have everlasting life in heaven.

The involvement of Jesus Christ in this battle is what actually gives man the power to overcome Satan. However, in spite of this, many people still end up in the place that was never intended for them by God - hell. Why is this so? The truth is that most people fail to recognize who their enemy is. They have been deceived, just as Adam and Eve were deceived to hand over the kingdom of man to Satan. The web of lies and deception of the enemy of mankind is too complex and sophisticated for man to comprehend. Human life span is not enough to study it but there is a simple way of bringing it to light through the word of God in the Bible.

We must understand first thing first that Satan or Lucifer or the devil and his messengers called demons or devils do exist. They are all immortal beings that are fighting mortal beings called man. When man dies, he only changes from mortality into immortality.

53

In the Epistle of Paul to the Ephesians chapter 6 verse 12, the Bible says, "For we do not wrestle against flesh and blood, but against principalities, against powers, against the rulers of the darkness of this age, against spiritual hosts of wickedness in the heavenly places."

From this passage, we can see the rank of the enemies of mankind. When a person declares himself for Christ in this battle, the first set of enemies he would face is called Principalities. Principalities operate mostly through human flesh. The very things that are contrary to the rules of survival in the battle are the ones principalities always influence Christians to get involved with. These principalities use the cravings for pleasure, materialism and things of this world to fight the Christians. That is why the word of God warns them in 1st Epistle of John chapter 2 verse 15, "Do not love the world or the things in the world. If anyone loves the world, the love of The Father is not in him. The Bible goes ahead to list the groups of principalities like lust of the flesh, lust of the eyes and the pride of life which you will find in the world.

Another reason Christians are warned against the love of the world is that the enemy - Satan has taken over almost all the areas of the kingdom of man with the primary aim of enslaving humanity and leading as many as are deceived and blindfolded to hell.

The next level of enemies of mankind is called Powers. These Powers are also in groups but I would only lists common ones and call them by names which you may be familiar with. They are Demonic Powers like powers of various secret cults, Political Powers, Psychological Power also known as Power of Brainwashing, Chemical Powers like the one that was used during world war 2 in Hiroshima in Japan, Economic Powers, Religious Powers and so many others like that.

The next level of enemies are the Rulers of Darkness which mostly design, manipulate and use human beings, situations and other things to rule the affairs of mankind. The Hosts Of Wickedness are the high level spirits that dictate to the Rulers of Darkness on the affairs of man.

The seats of powers, especially political and economic powers in most countries in the world are characterized with demonic symbols like design of the White House which was patterned with freemason symbols and the Illuminati logo in the $1 bill. This is one of the proofs that man is not really in charge of his governance. The Hosts Of Wickedness actually control the world through the Rulers Of Darkness. Hence, most political and other leaders are always involved in secret cultism. Any leader who is not a member of the secret cult like the Illuminati or Freemason or their puppets is either backed by God or gets eliminated or gets kicked out of the office. Let me prove this point with the quotations of some notable figures.

"The drive of the Rockefellers and their allies is to create a one-world government combining super capitalism and communism under the same tent, all under their control. Do I mean conspiracy? Yes, I do. I am convinced there is such a plot, international in scope, generations old in planning, an incredibly evil in intent." - Larry P. McDonald, US congressman in 1976, killed in the Korean Airlines 747 that was shot down by the Soviets.

"I care not what puppet is placed on the throne of England to rule the Empire... The man that controls Britain's money supply controls the British Empire. And I control the money supply." Baron Nathan Mayer de Rothschild.

"In politics, nothing happens by accident. If it happens, you can bet it was planned that way." - Franklin D. Roosevelt

"Ideas are more powerful than guns. We would not let our enemies have guns, why should we let them have ideas?" - Joseph Stalin.

"The high office of President has been used to foment a plot to destroy the American's freedom, and before I leave office I must inform the citizens of his plight." John F. Kennedy at Columbia University, 10 days before his assassination.

"It's not the votes that count, it's who counts the votes." - Joseph Stalin.

All these are just few out of so many quotations that prove man is not actually in charge of his affairs.

As a result of these enemies, man is forced into the battle he is not prepared to fight. The truth is: whether you know it or not, whether you believe it or not, whether you are a Christian or not, everybody is in the battlefield with lots of enemies that use things of this world to fight us, using human beings with political, economic, demonic, technological, psychological and other powers to fight us. They try to control our minds, driving most people out of their human senses, brainwashing and manipulating them to do what can ultimately destroy them.

When the enemies discover that man is waking up from the hypnotism that was injected into his mind, through one way or the other or one thing or the other, they create another web of lies or stupor to get him back to sleep. If religion is your soft spot, they create one for you. If materialism is your weakness, they sign a contract with you at the expense of your soul and make you forget what Jesus said in the Gospel according to Saint Matthew chapter 16 verse 26 when He asks everybody of the profit of a man who gains the whole world and loses his soul. If they discover that your soft spot is opposite sex, they will supply them to you because they have lots of them working for them. It is a sorrowful thing that so many Christians are falling victims, simply because they will not read the Bible, let alone to study it. So many ministers of God are getting frustrated everyday because people do not want to hear the word of God again. Most people had been brainwashed into rejecting the truth and accepting errors. Of course, we do not have to argue with errors. We can only attack them by publishing the truth. So this book is actually presented to you with the intention to attack errors, lies, deceptions, heresies and evils that have held mankind in bondage for so long. It is an attempt to resolve the issue of Insanity Of Humanity. I can only provide you with the truth in the word of God that will lead you to survival in this battle but I cannot enforce you to follow the way.

The Bible means everything to humanity. As I have it in one of my books titled: Network Bible Club Story book, the Bible is the map of the journey to eternity, the light for you to see in the dark, the picture of the nature of God, the mirror that shows if you're God's image, the answer to questions of children, the word that makes the wise see his folly, the sword with which Christians fight, the rod that put you right when you are wrong, the hammer that breaks the stony hearts and the book that stands out among other books.

These are all about the Bible and much more. To confirm if I am right about the book, please, first start reading the New Testament and study the life of Jesus Christ. You will note that when you meet with Jesus by reading the Bible, you will not remain the same. To encourage you to know Him personally is the principal motive of this book: The Insanity of Humanity.

After meeting with Jesus, the next few chapters suggest how you can develop a personal relationship with Him through Ministries Of Improvisations for yourself and family without interferences of brainwashed ministers who pose serious threats to so many spiritual and eternal lives.

CHAPTER FOURTEEN

THE CONCEPT OF MINISTRIES OF IMPROVISATIONS

Since the enemy of mankind has gone so far to wreck havoc on humanity, the concept of Ministries Of Improvisations becomes essential to consider for implementations by Christian individuals, families and schools. These ministries can be explained as ways of making up for the essential parts that are required for the survival of a Christian life in the world that is characterized by deceptions, lies, heresies and glamorous evils. Going by the results of this research work, most of the organized Churches and denominations have wrecked havoc into Christianity, conditioning the minds of the people to accept what God rejects, condone what God condemns and consider Christianity as a religion instead of a way of life as designed by God.

There are three basic types of Ministries Of Improvisations to be considered for implementations by people who have either become victims of brainwashing or religious abuses or just tending to have fellowship with God without any Church or denominational barricades. They are (1) The Home Church (2) School/Campus Fellowship (3) Office Fellowship.

The concept of Ministries Of Improvisations, especially The Home Church is borrowed from the concept of Homeschool. For background information, consider the extract from Mary Pride's Complete Guide To Getting Started in Homeschooling published by Harvest House Publishers in 2004. Mary Pride is a homeschool veteran.

HOMESCHOOL CONCEPT

"Homeschooling has some surprising benefits... As long as you're a committed parent with normal intelligence and no history of serious mental illness, homeschooling is the right choice for your child.

"You don't need an impressive educational background or lots of money to succeed at homeschooling. Research has shown that parents with only a high school education or less can do about as good a job as those with advanced degrees, or education degree.

58

"It has also shown that those who spend less than $200 per child per year on homeschool curriculum can get as good results as those who spend $400-$599 per child per year.

"Homeschooling yields positive academic, social, emotional, and spiritual benefits for any family that gives it an honest chance. By now it is no secret that all the research shows homeschooled children outstrip both their public and private school peers in every academic area.

"Years ago, strangers used to ask me, 'what about socialization?' Now, when I tell them I homeschool, they say, 'I don't blame you. The schools have become so dangerous!'

"As homeschooler, you won't have to worry about who is taking guns and knives to your local school. Your child also won't have to fear school bullies."

Now the question is: what is homeschool? An article culled in "We Stand For Homeschooling" in Mary Pride's Practical Homeschooling, printed in 2003, may shed light on this concept.

"The very nature, language and essence of homeschooling are being challenged and even co-opted by vast array of emerging educational programs which may be based in the home, but are funded by the government tax dollars, bringing inevitable government controls. These new "home-based" publicly-funded entities are variously called: charter schools, cyber-charters, e-schools, Independent Study Programs (ISP), Dual enrollment, Blended Schools Programs (BSP), Programs for Non-Public Students (PNPS), Public School Alternative Programs (PSAP), virtual schools, academies, community schools, home bond, and other newly devised terms and concepts.

"As that article goes on to say:

"There is a profound possibility that homeschooling is not only on the brink of losing its distinctiveness, but also in grave danger in losing its independence.

"The article cites stories from various sources to make this point:

"A school board member who likes 'the idea of using virtual school to reach out to families that want homeschooling for their children and refers to it as 'bringing home schooling under the state's umbrella.' This school set off loud alarm bells to any of us who value our educational freedom.

"A report from the Akron Beacom Journal, which states that 'educating children at home is fastest growing element of charter schools in the state' and reveals the profit motive behind such charter schools: 'While the schools receive $5,000 in the state and local money per child, the cost is only $2,500 per elementary pupil and $3,500 per high school schooler.' Big bucks to be made here, by both the charter school provider and the school district.

"An Education Week article reveals misbehavior on the part of a publicly funded charter school in Ohio. Such irregularities could lead to calls to regulate homeschooling, if charter schooling continues to be confused with homeschooling.

"We at PHS have always been happy to see parents getting more involved with their children's education... In one sense, teaching your children at home with public-school curriculum or a public-school online service is a step up. It certainly takes more parental involvement, and that is a good thing.

"So PHS is not questioning the value of online charter schools and other arrangements that public schools make which allows families to do some or all of their teaching at home. We just don't believe they should be called homeschools.

"Here is the definition of homeschooling:

"You and your child work together to pick resources including outside the home classes and learning adventures that will become your homeschool curriculum. You, the parent, teach some courses and supervise the rest.

"Key to this definition is that the parents, not school authorities, are in charge, and you have authority and ability to change the homeschool curriculum and schedule at any time. Surrendering authority and oversight to any school, tutor, organization, or individual is not homeschooling.

"Homeschooling is about educational freedom. It is not primarily about being at home..."

Now that you have an idea of what homeschooling is really all about, it instructive to consider the benefits which Mary Pride offered in her book, which is in line with the concept of Home Church.

According to her, homeschooling has safety benefits as well as emotional benefits.

"Six out of ten American teenagers witness bullying in school once a day or even more frequently, reported John A. Calhoun... released findings from a survey conducted by Wirthlin Worldwide that show that bullying is terrorist threat that most frightens America's teenagers and interferes with their education. Young people are far less concerned about external terrorist attacks on their schools and communities than they are about bully terrorizing them and their classmates in the hallways and classrooms of their schools.

"Most kids don't get their drugs at home. They get them at or near school...

"Emotional bullying-name calling, mockery, and humiliation can be just as devastating as physical bullying. Smart kids, special-needs kids, and anyone unlucky enough to appear 'different' can expect a steady diet of this negative emotional input in a typical school. Since research has shown that kids need to feel safe in order to learn, simply removing a child from the emotional pressure cooker of peer pressure, gangs, and cliques may produce enormous learning gains all by itself.

"According to a survey from National Campaign To Prevent Teen Pregnancy, 81 percent of kids aged 12-14 including those who have lost their chastity believe that kids today are pressured to have sex too early. Younger and younger kids are trying to dress and act sexy as well. Both school culture and sex-ed classes promote the idea that 'everybody is doing it' and that this is OK. And don't assume this is not true in your local Christian or Catholic school, unless the administration is making a real effort to keep things simple and sweet. In homeschool, parents can wait until their children are of reasonable age to learn the facts of life. At home, parents are also free to add morals and Scriptural teaching to the mix."

With the above findings of Mary Pride, it is noteworthy that to get freedom from the secular or spiritual strongholds over the family, Christian parents and teachers must be in charge of what their children or students learn.

The next chapter will share the concept of The Home Church.

CHAPTER FIFTEEN

THE CONCEPT OF THE HOME CHURCH

Having studied the concept of homeschool, which is mirrored in the Ministries Of Improvisations and since The Home Church bears some characteristics of organized Churches and denominations as distinguished from School/Campus and Office Fellowships, it will be discussed first and in a more elaborate form than any of the rest.

THE HOME CHURCH MINISTRY

The concept of The Home Church is inspired by what Jesus said in Matthew 18:20. "For where two or three (people or families) are gathered together in My Name, I am there in the mist of them."

A closer look at the organized religions at that time coupled with the attitudes of Pharisees and Sadducees who became the religious nuisances of their age while trying to make themselves relevant called for the assurance that no one needs to be part of any of any organized religions before he or she can really become a follower of Jesus Christ. The spirits behind organized religions in the days of Jesus Christ mastermind most of what we see in the organized Churches or denominations or religions in the modern days.

Results of the research works on why the Church is not effective in fighting the prevailing evils around the world indicate the followings:

1. The Church had become so big and organized that the enemy cannot miss his chance to bring it down. The fall of an elephant is easy. Standing on its feet again is the hard part. Various Churches and denominations had become so well organized that they are vulnerable to the infiltrations of anti-Christ spirits which operates at 4 different (M) levels, as I have it one of my books titled: The Age Of Anti-Christ Spirits. The levels are (i) Micro Level (ii) Mild Level (iii) Moderate Level and (iv) Major Level. The most deadly anti-Christ spirits in the Church today, according to the research works are the ones operating at Mild and Micro Levels.

They are most effective if the Church or the denomination that is well organized. They only need to operate through the leaders in a very mild or subtle form. It will take a Christian who is sound in the word of God, uncompromising and gifted with discerning Spirit before he can detect these anti-Christ spirits within the Church. These spirits are very good at planting destructive heresies in the midst of truths. A lie that is planted in the midst of truths is enough to mislead.

Most organized Church members would rather take so much of the Church doctrines that are outlined by their leaders either in the form of Bible Studies or Christian Education than taking the undiluted Word of God. I know of so many denominations that would follow their doctrines rather than what the Bible says even though there are obvious contradictions.

2. There is no Spirit of unity even among so many Christians and their leaders in the modern Church. This is caused by the dogmas of different Christian leadership, display of egos and strife. Most Christians are more loyal to their Church or denominations than to Christ to the extent that they almost consider other people who are not part of them as non-believers. My epic novel titled: "The Battle Of The Conquerors" paints a graphic picture of how the devil divides and rules most churches in this manner.

3. Most organized Churches and denominations had been hopelessly and thoroughly infiltrated by un-regenerated clergy, presenting various perverted versions of the original Church that was the real Body Of Christ.

With the above three out of many other issues which characterize so many modern Churches, it is unwise for people to be part of organized Church that have strayed away from the word of God, knowing fully well that if the devil is to attack or mislead anyone, he will first take away or dilute the pure word of God with heretical dogmas. Although some Churches still abide by the word of God but most of them have allowed ministers that are trained or deceived by anti-Christ spirits to lead them, going as far as infiltrating and subverting the congregations. Hence there is need for victims who are now skeptical about Christianity or the Church to improvise the Christian Fellowship by getting involved in a small unit of the larger Body Of Christ.

I would like to term the small unit of the Body Of Christ as follows: The Home Church or The House Church or The Family Church, although the only difference in all these is just the names. However, I would prefer to use the name The Home Church because of the term Home School.

I would define The Home Church as a congregation of two or more Christian families with friends in some cases in the home of one of the families, depending on the size of the meeting room. It appears many Churches and even denominations began as a Home Church Ministry but what actually went amiss is the inability to resist the temptation to get organized into a bigger congregation or Church or denomination. The meeting place is expected to determine when the unit is to break into two. If more people are getting involved in The Home Church, thereby stretching the meeting place, it is an indication to break into smaller units, not to get a bigger meeting place. The inability to resist the temptations to expand is where the concept usually transforms into a bigger Church or denomination with someone having the goal to sit as the overseer. In Acts 20:20, it was documented that Paul taught people the word of God publicly and from house to house.

The Home Church by the nature of its organization is autonomous though it is united with other Home Churches through: (1) The Spirit Of Christ (2) The Word Of God.

The Spirit Of Christ: Jesus told Peter in Matthew 16:18, "And I also say to you that you are Peter, and on this rock I will build My Church, and the gates of hell shall not prevail against it." After the death and resurrection of Jesus Christ, He commanded the people in Acts 1:4 to wait at Jerusalem for the promise of the Holy Spirit. Peter who was one of those who was to later build the congregation of believers called Church was with other disciples of Jesus Christ in one accord in a house, according to Acts 2:1-4. They became filled with the Holy Spirit that came down from heaven. From then, the people began to congregate to hear the word of God, growing big and doing things in common, according to Acts 2:40-47. There are lots of things the Church have to contend with in their age. First, the religious system needs to change before it can accommodate Christianity. Of course, change does not come so easy. So martyrdom of Christians is the commonest price before

Christianity began to get a firm grip over the people even up to the Dark Age for Christians. The disciples, including Peter in Acts 10:24-33 held services from house to house. God used the instrument of persecution in Act 8:1-4 to prevent the Church from getting so organized into what we have in the modern days. According to that passage, persecution was also used to make the word of God spread all over the world up to the time the Church found itself in a comfort zone where and when the leadership decided that there should be a universal Church. Getting so organized is never the concept of God, going by the Acts of the Apostles.

In the book of Revelation, Jesus identified various Churches by their geographical locations, not by names of their denominations. The epistles of Paul are usually addressed by the nationality names like the epistles to the Hebrew, Thessalonians or the names of the person he was addressing.

Having said these, it is instructive to note that The Home Church is a concept from God as long as it is bore by the Spirit of Christ who founds the Church. The victims of the spiritual misdeeds and abuses of some organized Churches can come together to form The Home Church, starting with their families in their homes instead of feeling frustrated or suspicious of other Churches that may want them to join their congregations. After all the ultimate goal of any Christian or Church is to make heaven.

Some of the ways Christians can prove that they are serious about going to heaven are: (i) To obey the word of God after being born-again. (1 Peter 1:22-23) (ii) To congregate as a Body of Christ as instructed in Hebrew 10:25 (iii) To worship God in the truth and the Spirit (John 4:24) (iii) To tell others about Jesus Christ (Mark 16:15-18) (iv) To pray constantly (1Thessalonians 5:17) and (v) to be the light of the world through good works, conduct and attitude towards everybody including their enemies. (Matthew 5:14-16)

<u>The Word Of God:</u> Just as a Christian must abide by the word of God before he can reach the kingdom of God, The Home Church must abide by the word of God. The guiding principles of The Home Church are in the Bible. All the programmes of The Home Church, including singing, teaching, preaching and praying which are what all Churches have in common must be in line with the

Bible. Going by this Biblical concept, apparently, at least a minister is required in The Home Church. Hence, there are some career ministers who may see this as opportunities to be engaged in the ministry of The Home Church. This may be a good idea if the minister is really godly and sound in the word of God, having the right motive. However, everybody must be informed that Jesus Christ does not come into the world to give anyone a career but to reconcile the world to God, the Father of all. Besides that, it MUST be noted that every genuine Christian is called to be a minister (Romans 8:28-30). A Christian is either called to be a Bible teacher or a Pastor etc (1Corinthians 12:28-31). The general calling of all Christians is evangelism as recorded in Mark 16:15-20. The ministries of healing, deliverance, teaching and preaching are embedded in the general ministry of evangelism, according to that passage. It is true that some Christians may need training before they can really be effective in the pasturing of some Churches, especially big ones but The Home Church is easy enough to handle. In fact, all the leader of The Home Church needs is to be filled with the Holy Spirit and to study the whole Bible personally or with the families. Through that he or she would learn on the job.

It must be noted that it is better to use the most fervent member of the family who is filled with Spirit of God and a little vast in the scriptures as the leader of the Home Church than to risk having an outsider whose background is unknown as the Pastor. There are, however, some ministers and missionaries who sincerely desire to do the work of the Lord even for free because they know that all souls are very precious to God.

The instruction that brings about the congregation of people of God is found in Hebrew 10:25 but barricades are established in most of the organizations of modern Churches and denominations. Such barricades, which invariably fence out so many people out of the Church, include the followings:

(I)   Strife to lead the Church or group. A lot of people lord themselves over others just as this had been pointed out in 1 Peter 5:2-4. The bigger the Church, the more the strife or problems associated with it. There so many cases of strife among Church, group and other leaders, including the ones in the so-called associations of Christians.

(II) Politics in the Church. The way some ministers use the pupils to buy into the hearts of the people rather than to direct their minds to God is shocking. I have seen a youth leader hijacking a Church from a Pastor because his leadership style did not go down well with him. The position of a leader of so many Churches had become elected post. We all know what happens when a person is elected into a position. He will be made to serve those who elect him there, not God who calls him to lead.

(III) The issue of finances is another serious issue for the organized Church to contend with. Naturally, money has a way of attracting everybody, including the wolves in sheep skins. Knowing the wolves among the leaders is a problem because they are all good at pretending. A lot of people claim to be called into the ministries by God but the truth is that they want to serve their bellies.

The Home Church cannot face all these problems because, for one, the family members involved are familiar with one another. Secondly, they can readily predict each other. Even if there is a black sheep in the family, he or she cannot hide from others who would learn to tolerate and pray for him. After all, an adage says, 'the devil you're familiar with is better than the angel you do not know.'

However, there will be some challenges The Home Church is likely to face. The followings are likely going to be issues to face. I suggest how to handle each of them.

1. The issue of the leadership may be a challenge as there may not be someone fervent enough to man the leadership position in the Home Church. The congregation of the families may do either of these: (i) allow a good Christian they can trust to put them through the normal basic programmes until they get a member among the families who can lead them or (ii) engaged the service of missionary or other minister who may lead them as long as they want.

2. The financial challenge which organized Churches always face needs to be addressed by The Home Church for the mere fact that tithes and offerings would need to be collected for the following reasons as mandated by God in Malachi 3:8-12: (a) They are used to bless visiting ministers or missionary who blessed the

congregation spiritually (Numbers 18:21-24). (b) They are also used to bless widows and the orphans (Deuteronomy 14:28-29). (c) They are used to organize programmes, such as inviting friends for dinner during special occasions (Deuteronomy 14:22-26) and (d) they can be used to buy Bibles and teaching materials that bless and edify the people. Once everybody understands what tithes and offerings are meant for, there would be no problem of misappropriations. The idea is: God's money must be spent God's way.

3. One of the major challenges of Lay Ministers or Missionaries is planning of usual or special programmes. This can easily be overcome if The Home Church keeps its normal and other programmes short and simple, emphasizing only the basic things like (i) Opening Prayers (ii) Praise And Worship/Special Numbers (iii) Reading of Bible/Studies (iii) Sermon (iii) Collections Of Tithes And Offerings To The Lord (iv) Announcements and (v) Closing Prayers. As brief as these programmes may seem, it may take more hours to carry out, especially if other activities are included.

4. There are special activities, which may be complicated to Lay Ministers or Missionaries such as Holy Communion Service and Water Baptism but a close study of how it was done in the Bible, especially in the Acts of Apostles and studies of other books in that regards will give them insight. One unique thing about Home Church is the unity among the families. Hence, fault finders that pose as bullies will hardly show up. This makes it easy for the Home Church leaders to learn more on the job. The small size of the Home Church also makes it easy for the leaders to operate and delegate assignments to others.

It is instructive to note, however, that the above suggestions may not work in every part of the world or country. Hence, there is need for the Missionary who may wish to assist various families to plant Home Church to study the environment, culture and the legal system of the country before he or she customize or improvise for the things that may be amiss in these suggestions.

CHAPTER SIXTEEN

THE CONCEPT OF SCHOOL/CAMPUS/OFFICE FELLOWSHIPS

This may not really be a new concept since Fellowships already exist in many places, including offices, schools and campuses. To categorize and study the concept of these Fellowships, however, there is need to define it.

A Fellowship, as distinguished from a Church, is the gathering of Christians with the sole objective to worship God and share the word of God within the available time. Thus there are various types of Fellowships but our focus is on (i) Primary School Fellowship (ii) Secondary School Fellowship (iii) Campus Fellowship and (iii) Office Fellowship.

Before we begin the study of each of them, it is instructive to note that the concept of each Fellowship may not work the same way everywhere. So the missionary or minister who wants to implement any of the concepts in order to meet the spiritual needs of the people may need to find out if it will work.

I have had the privileges to train and equip missionaries with materials which are used to plant Bible Clubs and School Fellowships in Nigeria. Such materials include Foundation Bible Club Story Books for children of all age groups in primary schools and Network Bible Club Story Books for Secondary School, Campus and office Fellowships. There are lectures for teachers, parents, missionaries and other ministers inside each volume. The effects of these books are parts of what inspire me to gather more materials for teachings. There are many other good books for ministrations by seasoned ministers which can also serve this purpose.

PRIMARY SCHOOL FELLOWSHIP

The misleading or wrong information that characterize this age makes this type of Fellowship crucial in every part of the world. Any school that is serious about making positive impact on their pupils needs to establish this Fellowship. With the findings of various researchers, a lot of damage had been done to the psyches of humanity through means of education, information and entertainments. This invariably paved way for crimes right in the schools that are meant to groom godly leaders. Private and other schools can make a difference by establishing these Fellowships; thereby improvising for all that are required to add moral values to their students. There are two ways of doing this. They are: (i) Introduction of Christian Moral Instructions as a subject into the school curriculum. The materials in Foundation Bible Club Story Books can serve this academic purpose and at the same time boost the spiritual and moral values of the students with or without the use of other books. (ii) Establishment of School Bible Club Fellowship. A Children Bible Teacher or Missionary may be required to use the book or Calvary Rock Resources Booklets to coordinate the Fellowship every week within a set time. The programmes of some of the Fellowships that are planted in Primary and Secondary Schools in Nigeria by Calvary Rock Resources can provide a guide. They are as follows: 1. Praise and worship 2. Opening prayers 3. Revision of the previous lessons. 4. Special number or song or drama presentation if any. 4. Story and Bible lessons in the story for the week. 5. Class activities. 6. Prayers 7. Offerings if the school permits it. (The offerings are used to acquire teaching materials or used to organize special programs for members of the School Bible Club each term.) 8. Closing Prayers.

The Bible Club Fellowship concept can also fit into Homeschool, involving children from other homeschools.

SECONDARY OR HIGH SCHOOL FELLOWSHIP

There is an article by Exhort-Ezine titled: "Should God's People Send Their Kids To Satan's School?" The article reads as follows:

"If Satan were to run a school, how would it run it?

"First - Satan would make an absolute law that no knowledge of the true God of the Bible can be taught. Not only could God not be talked to, He couldn't talk to anyone either. No prayers.

"Any religious teaching in Satan's schools must be about other gods.

"Second - in Satan's school, the basis of all instructions must be the religious belief that there is no Creator: that all creations happened by chance, that mankind was not special creation by God, that he is just one with the worms and monkeys. Evolution.

"Following this theory, Satan would teach that mankind is subject only to the same law as the worms and monkeys. Since we came from slime, we can act like slime. Unbridled breeding and sodomy are not sins, just different animal behaviours. In Satan's schools, ten commandment moralities must never be imposed.

"Third - Satan's schools must be chocked full of fruits of Satan's way of life - destructive sex, vicious fits of violence, and mind killing drugs. Such things as girls wearing skirts up to their butts and blouses down to their breasts. Or kids being able to get drugs more easily in the school halls than on the city streets. And mindless massacres, where young lives are blown to bits by other kids.

"Wait a minute - I have just described the American public schools. They are run just the way Satan would run a school. That means America public schools are Satan's school."

This writer may sound blunt but he was able to back up his points with cases and references to American Law and Government policies.

Having established the fact that young minds are designed to be what they are by the environmental and other factors, it also vital to add moral values into them by establishing Fellowships in High Schools or include Christian Moral Instructions so as to make up their spiritual needs. Network Bible Club Story Book which has similar materials to Foundation Bible Club Story Book is designed to serve these purposes. It is designed for both youths of all age groups and adults. Thus the programmes designed for Primary School Fellowship can be applicable.

CAMPUS FELLOWSHIP

Again this is not a new concept but most of Campus Fellowships are dependent or affiliated to the organized Churches, making them to face similar challenges. The only notable difference is the elections of new leaders almost every year as they graduate from the school.

To avoid the same challenges of most organized Churches or

denominations, which many Fellowships must have inherited, there is need to modify the concept. It needs to take the pattern of The Home Church with few modifications like: (i) instead having families, there will be friends that form a big family that congregate in a room that is big enough to accommodate the members. (ii) Though in Home Church, the leader may not need to be changed; there will always be a change of leadership in Campus Fellowship as the students graduate from school.

Aside from the above, all others things, including the programmes in The Home Church can be applied or modified for implementations.

OFFICE FELLOWSHIP

This concept is not new as well. It is applicable among many Christian workers and professionals. The mode of operations is relatively simple enough. I was privileged to be the Chaplin of the National Electric Power Authority Christian Fellowship in Ilorin District Office when I was a civil servant in 1997 in Nigeria. We usually meet for Fellowship during office break for 1 hour every working day. Others in other Districts meet only twice or trice a week. The design of the programmes is simple enough. We have no reason to be involved in finances unless we are embarking on building of our meeting place within the office, which we never completed before I retired as a civil servant. Since we did not have issues with money, there is no problem of finances or even administrations. The programmes usually go this way: (i) Opening Prayers (ii) Praise And Worship (iii) Sermon (iv) Collection of offerings (*which are usually used to print tracts or buy Bibles for non-Christians in the office or plan yearly programmes with the aim of bringing new people within the office into the Fellowship etc*) (v) Announcement and (iv) Closing prayers.

It is made so simple that within 1 hour, the programmes are over.

If Christians working in offices that observe recess give this concept a chance, they tend to be successful. It will be in their records that they impact their environments.

CHAPTER SEVENTEEN

MISSIONARY AND EVANGELISTIC MINISTRIES IN THE HOME CHURCH, SCHOOL, CAMPUS, OFFICE FELLOWSHIPS AND OTHER PLACES

There has never been so much need of evangelists and missionaries in the history of mankind as it is in the modern days. Missionary fields are now so much and broad that there can never be enough workers to harvest the fields. As defined in the previous chapters, the fields extend to schools, homes, offices and everywhere. As if the missionary fields are not plenty enough, some Churches that are supposed to be involved in preserving the souls till the second coming of the Lord are adding more to the missionary works, stretching the insufficient manpower resources beyond limit. Their operations are seriously thwarting the efforts of others to reach out and preserve souls for eternity. Yet missionary works and evangelism are the assignments of all matured Christians, not for angels in heaven who also have their own assignments.

Before we discuss few things about the works and the reasons every Christian must be involved in either missionary works or evangelism or both, I want you to consider one of the children stories titled "The House On Fire" in Young Generation Bible Club Story Book, the Volume 2 of Foundation Bible Story Book, which reads:

"There is a man who builds a very big house and put all his children inside. Although the children are so many but the house is big enough to accommodate them. As the number of the children increased, they become more and more uncomfortable. There are always problems in the house. Many of them do not love each other. So they fight one another, steal each other's things and harm one another. The man decides to go to another place to build beautiful mansion for each one of them.

"One day, when he is away to the place to prepare the mansions, fire broke out in that house. Most of the children do not know that there is fire in the house. So they keep enjoying themselves, eating,

73

drinking and doing other things. Some of those who know about the fire do nothing about it, thinking, "Father would soon come to take us to the mansions in another place." Some of those who manage to escape are too joyful to border about the rest. They say to themselves, "wao! We escape from the fire! Let Father come to take us to our new home now."

"Many other children are compassionate enough to warn others in the house about the fire, doing all they can to help many to get out of the house. If all the children that escape are helping others to get out of the house, so many of them would not be burnt to death. But most of them are not. So the man finds only few children to take to the new home. He becomes very sorrowful because he does not want to lose any of his children.

"The story is talking about Jesus and you. Jesus is the Father that goes to prepare mansions for His children in heaven. This world is the house that is full of many problems. All the people in this world are the children in the house and the fire is hell where all those who commit sins will go unless they are born-again. Those who escape from the fire are those who are born-again. Those who help others to escape from the fire are those who are telling others to stop committing sins while the rest are those do not care whether people go to hell or not. Who are you among these children?"

Penn Jillete, an American atheist, illusionist and comedian said, *"I don't respect people who don't proselytize (in Christian term: evangelize) ... If you believe that there's a heaven and hell and people could be going to hell and not getting eternal life or whatever, and you think that it's not really worth telling them this because it would make it socially awkward ... How much do you have to hate somebody to believe that everlasting life is possible and not tell that?"*

To illustrate the point Penn is trying to make, let us imagine a little child who is crawling across the highway with cars speeding ahead of him while you stand by the road, watching him. Even though you have the chance to save the child, if you do nothing to get him out of the road, it is plain wickedness. If you watch the car crushing the child, you are responsible for his death. What Penn is saying in essence is that if you believe heaven and hell exist and you don't try to warn people about the places in any way you can, you either do not believe there is hell or you are just being hateful.

Before giving my life to Christ, I was a real controversial sinner who knew how to argue against eternal life but one lady prayed for me in her closet that God should arrest me. So when I slept one fateful night, my spirit left my body and I found myself facing a long queue, where we are being judged. When it was my turn, I was condemned to hell according to Revelation 21:8. Just as I was heading to hell, Jesus, the joy and the hope of the world came to me and told me He is giving me the last chance to mend my ways. I came back to life as a changed person.

About 10 years later, I was fed up with life. I told God that I want to come home in heaven. Again, I found myself going to heaven but before I reached the gate which had been opened to me, multitudes of people blocked my way. They all pointed accusing fingers at me, saying that it was unfair and unjust if I go to heaven while they end up in hell. At the gate of heaven, I discovered that sin is not the only thing that prevents a person from getting to heaven but sinners can also stop a Christian if he does not preach to them. Ever since then, I've been involved in massive evangelism through publications, films, music, media and other means of communicating the word of God.

With the above illustrations and personal experience, there is need to study the basic ministries of all Christians. I will just focus on few most important things. I recommend that matured Christians get details on this issue in one of my books titled: Successful Christianity And Basic Ministries.

The first thing to note in the basic ministries of all Christians is that souls are hanging on their necks as they shy away from the assignments to reach out to them with the word of God. The only way they can relieve themselves of these burdens is to perform the assignments, which are:

Evangelism through works of their faith (James 2:14-22), words of their mouths or their testimonies (Revelation 12:11) as in the case of a woman who met Jesus by the well in John 4:6-30. The case of this woman proves that if you are born-again today, you can be an evangelist today. What matters is the zeal to share your faith and reach out to others.

Discipleship of others who just come to the knowledge of Christ, which is known as missionary works today is crucial. (Colossians 1:

28-29, Mark 16:15- 20).

With the fields that are available now, no one has reason to be idle in the service of the Lord. The Bible says in Proverbs 11: 30 that he who wins soul is wise. If you consider what many people, including some Christians are seeking for at the expense of their souls, you will understand the level of foolishness if not insanity of man. Consider the parable of Jesus Christ about the rich fool in Luke 12:13-21.

Reasons which many Christians give for not getting involved in evangelism or missionary works include the followings:

1. Lack of time. Consider the experience in my encounter with a wealthy friend, which I wrote in a Calvary Rock Resources tract titled: Encounter With A Rich Man. This will answer the question of time. It reads:

   He was not particularly pleased to see me because he has the impression that I was a religious fanatic. He could not turn me away; not after he had agreed to at least listen to what I've got to say.

   He was my friend and a rich man too. His single problem was that his riches have gotten into his head.

   "As you are aware," he told me just as I was ushered into his luxurious office, "I have no time to burn. So I will appreciate it if you go right straight to the point."

   "If death knocks at the door now, you won't be too busy to die; would you?" I asked, sitting in front of him.

   "I'm very healthy and too young to die, you realize that."

   I smiled courteously. "I had that thought sometime ago," I told him in a very polite way. I have learnt to be very polite whenever I am about to point out hideous facts. "But I got a better idea when I visited the mortuary. I've seen countless dead bodies in my life and I have even found out the causes of their deaths. My conclusion was that death has no respect for age, sex, status, health or whatever. Anybody can die at anytime and at anywhere and can be killed by anything. You remember a few of our friends who have promising careers in those days but, as you know, they are now in the grave. We've got only one chance to live and only today to think of. You can have all the pleasures you want in this world but what happens when you die. As a matter of fact, I'm here to warn you of what lies ahead of you if you die without Christ. Think of it, my friend. What have you got to gain if you gain the whole wide world and go to hell and what have you got to lose if you lose the pleasure of the world for the sake of Christ?"

I leaned over to him to continue in a whisper. "If you miss that place called heaven, you will cry in agony. I will not be there to hear you. But if you become born-again like me and endure all sorts of names I've had to endure, we'll laugh together in heaven where there is no pain or sorrow."

I leaned backward again and smiled at him as he looked thoughtful. "No matter how much you have acquired in this world, you won't take anything with you when you die, would you? Somebody else will have to inherit all you have worked so hard to acquire." In a very gentle voice, I asked the question that means a lot to everybody. "Do you want to be born-again and go to heaven when you depart from this world? Or you want live in sin and die again in hell? The choice is yours to make. I have delivered the message God has for you. Your blood is cleared off my neck."

There was a long uncomfortable silence. Then he said with sober reflection, "you are my best friend and I don't even know it."

I smiled wearily. At least, he heard me. "Do you want us to pray now? I have other people to see."

2. <u>Lack of experience or resources:</u> One thing about the work of the Lord, you do not need any experience or funds before you can start. What you need is the conviction, which brings about zeal. God always train His people to be ministers while doing the job, not even in Bible schools. I acquired virtually all my experiences on the job as I am involved in our ministries and through the experiences of others that are compiled in books and audio messages. Besides, there are many materials like books published by Calvary Rock Resources that can be used by anyone, including a child for evangelism and missionary works. A 10 year old pupil used Foundation Bible Club A-Z Story Book to do missionary work in a primary school that was founded by an Atheist in Nigeria. If that is so, the question of lack of experience or funds is not tenable before God. Calvary Rock Resources has designed lots of materials for missionary works in Primary, Secondary,

Campus Fellowships, Home and other Churches worldwide. I am sure there are other materials by other Christian organizations for these purposes. Hence, a Christian who is ready to perform missionary assignments or be involved in evangelism should be ready to study the Bible and others books that can be used to minister to the spiritual needs of others.

3. <u>Lack of audience:</u> A lot of Christians complain that people would not listen to them, especially when they discover that they are trying to convert them into Christianity. Again this is not tenable before God. What I observe in the life of people who present this as an excuse is found in what Penn Jillete said about not evangelizing because it is socially awkward. They often feel embarrassed when people ignored or tried to shut them up when sharing the Gospel. Every Evangelist knows it is not easy to win souls for Christ. Some missionaries have to give up their lives before they can reach others. I read the story of a free man who gave himself to be sold as a slave so that he could reach out to the slaves. If a Christian discovers that it cost Jesus His Glory, Dignity in Heaven, water, blood in His Body and His life on earth to deliver mankind from bondage; he will be willing to sacrifice whatever it takes to make souls for Christ. There are pulpits in every walk of life, schools, homes, streets - everywhere for Christians to reach out for souls. They can do that through distribution of printed materials in schools, streets and even offices. It is not the function of a Christian to convict a person of his or her sins but rather to preach the word of God through whichever avenue he has chosen. The word of God that is delivered to the person would be used either to save him from eternal death or be used against him on the Day of Judgment.

In conclusion, it must be understood that the more the maturity of a Christian, the more productive he is expected to be. Jesus likened a Christian to a branch of tree in John 15:1-8. If Christians do not abide in Him, they would be cut off and thrown inside fire. If they abide in Him, they will produce fruits. One of the greatest proofs that Christians abide in Jesus Christ is in their services and productivity.

Having studied this book up to this final chapter, you need to understand that you are almost a minister if not yet a minister that will be involved in evangelism and missionary works in the streets, place of work or school or at Home Church. What you need to do now is to begin or continue to grow in Christ just like other Christians. There is no limit to spiritual growths. In fact, the moment a Christian stops growing, he starts dying. The books that are introduced to you in the next few pages are to either help you grow spiritually or equip you to be productive.

CHECK OUT OTHER BOOKS BY DIPO TOBY ALAKIJA
Each Serves Either As Edifying Or Evangelical Or Missionary or Academic Tool At Home, School, Bible Clubs, Sunday Schools, Church, Office And Other Fellowships

CHRISTIAN MINISTRIES AND BASIC LEADERSHIP
ISBN: 978-36348-7-9 ISBN: 978-978-36348-7-9
A Collection Of Resource Materials That Follows Up Successful Christianity And Basic Ministries Course Book

As it is common to say that the hood does not make a monk, the dignified positions and bogus titles of many Christian leaders in modern days do not really make them Gospel Ministers.

This course book - a compilation of five resource materials on Missions And Outreach Ministries, Christian Communication Arts, Christian Leadership, Christian Education Methodology and Ministries Of Improvisations - aims at making every matured Christian an effective minister and leader at their respective homes, communities and nations. It teaches various ways Christians can communicate the word of God, meeting up to their responsibilities as ministers and leaders that reconcile people to God, edifying the Body Of Christ and reaching out to souls at the same time.

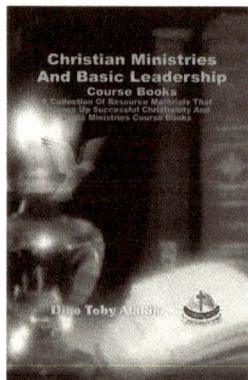

All of the resource materials are in use in Bible Schools like College Of Christian Education And Missions, in Churches and other ministries to raise Christian workers, Evangelists, Missionaries and other Ministers that serve at various levels and leadership capacities.

FOOTSTEPS IN THE MUD
ISBN: 978-36348-9-5 ISBN: 978-978-36348-9-3
The Drama Package Of Results Of Research Works That trace Global And Societal Vices To The Corrupt Or Lost Of Family Values

The 13-Episode drama book involves Bosede who learnt many wrong things from her parents' conduct and foul language. She was forced to marry Kola when she became pregnant. Using her mother's method to handle her father, she tried to subject Kola to her control. In the course of that, she made life terrible for him. Although her mother tried to warn her of the implications of maltreating her husband but Bosede has grown out of control. Consequently, while looking for peace, Kola was pushed out of the house. He made friends with some guys who taught him the unholy ways of life and influenced him to become a menace in the house.

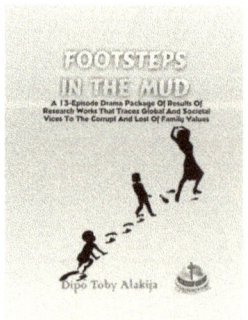

Junior who was born at time the couple never proved to be responsible parents also learnt wrong things from them. He decided to follow his father's footsteps by taking alcohol when he was in primary school. As if that was not bad enough, he tried to teach other children in the school the madness in his home. A school teacher, however, was able to influence him and his mother by teaching them Christian morals. Even then, Junior was soon caught in the crossfire at home as his father tried to enlist him as a future member of a secret cult that posed as a social club.

SUCCESSFUL CHRISTIANITY AND BASIC MINISTRIES
ISBN: 978-49874-6-0
A Collection Of Resource Materials That Precedes Christian Ministries And Basic Leadership Course Book

The first question is how Christianity is practiced even in a hostile environment. Next to that is the question about the potentials of Christians in spite of their apparent limitations. The other issues are connected to the successes, deliverance, callings, basic ministries of all Christians and evangelism. Various schools of thoughts have attempted these questions but many answers only portray Christianity as a form of religion instead of a way of life as specified by God. Some answers give room for compromise, hypocrisies, dogmas and denominational doctrines. The misconceptions about these areas of Christianity have brought about worldliness instead of righteousness and false achievements instead of fulfillment.

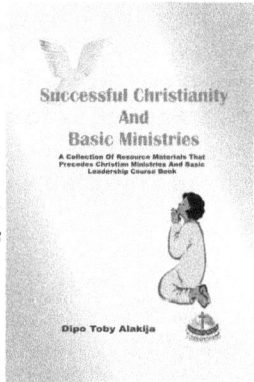

This book which contains six different subjects had been used to hold seminars at various levels, train ministers and Christian workers in Bible Schools and to equip the Church. It explains in simple terms the seemingly complex issues on practice of Christianity, Potentials, Deliverance, God's Kind Of Success, Evangelism and Basic Ministries of a Christian with Biblical principles, life transforming stories and illustrations.

NO MORE TEARS TO SHED
ISBN: 978-49874-3-0 ISBN: 978-978-74-3-1

Kidnappers took Tokunbo away from his grand parents in a city in Nigeria when he was a little boy. A nice woman found him in another town and gave him a false identity. She spoilt him with love, making him to grow into a rebellious teenager that was not appreciated anywhere. When Janet made him a Christian, however, life began to make sense to him until the day he was beaten to the point of death for the offence he knew nothing about. He left the town

for the city which, unknown to him, held his true identity and the link to his parents in the United States. To find them was only a question of time.

THE UNROMANTIC LOVE BIRDS
ISBN: 978-4987-5-7 ISBN: 978-978-4974-5-5
And other short stories about love and marriages

They were very much in love right from their school days but when they got married and had children, romance became the game Charles' wife refused to play. No matter how much he tried to make her understand the unbearable condition her unromantic attitude has subjected him into, she would not change. Consequently, after enduring for so long, he was forced to look for the women that would make up for her weakness. He unofficially married a beautiful lady of insane jealousy. Though she was ready to give him what was missing in his marriage, it soon dawn on him that he has solved one big problem only to create a bigger one.

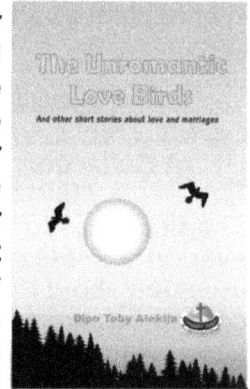

THE BATTLE OF THE CONQUERORS
ISBN: 978-49874-7-3 ISBN: ISBN: 978-978-49874-0-7-9

Wickedness takes over the land of Bondage from First Couple and subjects everybody into slavery without giving anybody the chance to be free. Love brings The Redeemer from Eternity and offers the slaves the chance to escape. Wickedness soon declares war and engages everyone in the battle. The Redeemer makes the redeemed people Conquerors by giving them the armour of war and Comforter but Wickedness cannot be undone. He has several thousands of years of experience in the war. So he is quick to recognize the weakness of the redeemed people who are ignorant of their strengths and advantages. Although the Conquerors fight like immutable giants, rescuing victims of war, many people suffer heavy casualties.

Since King Wickedness knows that a redeemed person is strong enough to chase one thousand of his warriors at a time, and two would put ten thousand into flight, he enlists as one of his warriors the people's deadliest enemy called Disunity.

Wickedness is able to strike the people by making them to fight with one another, turning what is supposed to be their best moments in the battle into tales of woes.

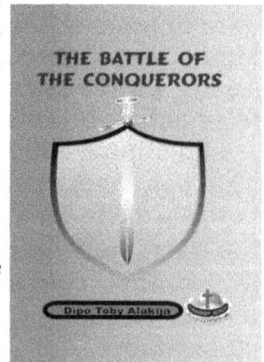

BLOODSHED IN CAMPUS

ISBN: 978-07350-3-8 ISBN: 978-978-07350-3-6

A poor widow tearfully warned her son, Richard, against joining the bad wagon when he got an admission into one of the Nigerian Universities. He resisted the membership of groups of students, including the Christian Fellowship until he had an encounter with a member of The Black Skulls - a deadly and ruthless secret cult on the campus.

Before Richard knew what he was up against, the head of The Black Skulls had arranged items for his initiation into the cult. While resisting being initiated, he ran to the Christian Fellowship for help. The leader of the Christian Fellowship dragged The President of Students' Union Government (S.U.G) into the conflict. With the involvement of the S.U.G President, another formidable cult called The Red Eyes felt obliged to team up against The Black Skulls. Then the campus turned into a battlefield and BLOODSHED became the order of the black day.

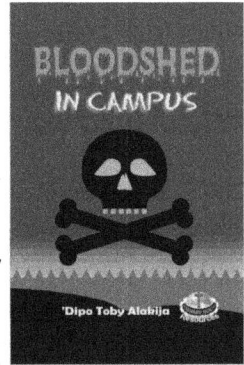

NETWORK BIBLE CLUB
YOUTH AND ADULT BOOK ONE

ISBN: 978 - 978- 49874-9-X ISBN: 978-978-49874-9-3

A collection of 26 life transforming stories, 26 poems, 26 hymn tuned songs and weekly Bible lessons

The issue of moral instructions in schools and at homes is threatened with extinction. Consequently, so many youths are involved in prostitution, drug addictions, cultism, fraudulent practices, armed robberies and other crimes. Those who are supposed to be trained as leaders in various walks of life are the ones posing serious threats to many lives. Many parents who fail to add moral values to the upbringing of their children often times breed potential criminals under their roofs without knowing it. Apart from these, many other people negatively influence young ones through the media, music, publications, films, conduct and foul language; making them to lose their moral and family values.

This book one just like the rest of other volumes is an attempt to bring back moral instructions into schools and campuses through the use of stories, hymn tuned songs, poems, Bible lessons and class activities. It is designed to assist teachers and ministers in Secondary Schools, Bible Clubs, Churches and Campus Fellowships to teach people, especially youths the Word of God and serves as a school text book in subjects relating to literature, music and other creative works.

FOUNDATION BIBLE CLUB A-Z STORY BOOK

ISBN: 978-49874-2-2 ISBN: 978-978-49874-2-4

Volume 1 With 26 Stories, 26 Bible

Lessons, 26 Rhymes And 26 Songs For Book For Young Minds

An adage says, "a man who builds a house without building his child builds what the child will later sell." Proverbs 22:6 says, "train up a child in the way he should go: and when he is old, he will not depart from it." This book is an attempt to assist parents and teachers to meet up to the challenges that befall them in carrying out this important function in the light of the moral decadence that is prevailing all over the world.

The first edition of the book was used by several thousands of teachers, ministers and parents in schools, Churches and homes to build the moral values of young ones. Apart from the stories, songs and Bible passages for the young ones to study, there is a seminar material that is based on the lecture which the author delivered to school proprietors, children ministers and Christian professionals in this volume.

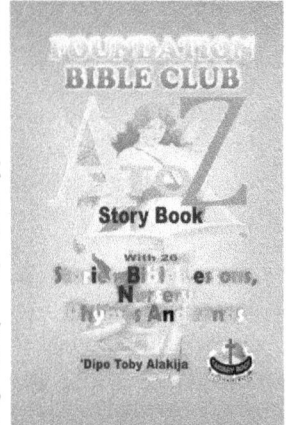

RANSOM FOR LOVE

ISBN: 978-49874-8-1 ISBN: 978-978-4987-4-8-6

She accepted his marriage proposal without knowing the kind of person he was. She soon discovered that he was a mean and ruthless guy who was always ready to get whatever he wanted by all means even if he has to pay for it with the lives of others. She was in his bondage, especially when her parents who believed he was a generous and gentleman were on his side.

Because she considered the proposal to marry him as a marriage engagement with the devil incarnate, she decided that she would rather die than to share her life with him. Then out of the blues, this passionate gentleman sneaked into her life despite all she did to discourage him. She could not resist his love for her when he offered to set her free from the devil incarnate. Then the battle began – sooner than they anticipated.

THE WEIGHT OF DEATH
ISBN: 9978-36348-0-1 ISBN: 978-978-36348-0-0
(Story Of The Spirit Eyes Series)

PLAY ONE: HORROR IN THE FAMILY: Talimi probably did not envisage his death when he was trying to compel his son, Damola to succeed him in the occult Brotherhood. Other members of the secret cult were aware of the battle between them. So when Talimi died; his family, especially Damola who was a diehard Christian began to fall prey to the cult. Using all their powers and the spirit that posed as Talimi's ghost, the cult waged war against the family, tormenting and making them to be at loggerheads.

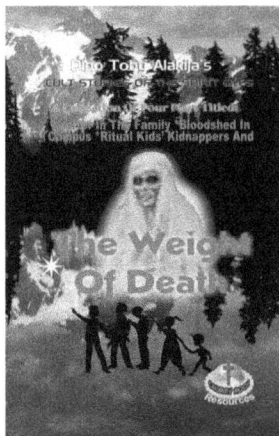

PLAY TWO: RITUAL KIDS' KIDNAPPERS: Victor and the rest of the members of the School Bible Club were taught that there are lots of evil people in this world but he did not understand why God allowed him to be among the children that were taken away from their parents. He soon understood that he was to be used by God to rescue other children who did not know that everyone that truly believes in Jesus has the power to overcome evil.

PLAY THREE: THE WEIGHT OF DEATH: Awoseun would not have known the real source of problems of mankind if his father had not given him the power to see demons tormenting the people in different ways. What he was yet to know, however, was the power of light over darkness. When he was caught in crossfire between these powers, he desperately sought for deliverance.

CALVARY ROCK RESOURCE BOOKLETS
ISSN: 1595 93X
The Quarterly Missionary Booklets That Are Designed To Teach Children, Youths And Adults In Schools, Fellowships, Churches, At Homes, Office And Other Places.

Although all the various volumes of this booklet can be used independently of other books but it is recommended that it should be used as part of supplementary materials to make up for Foundation and Network Bible Club Story Books for both children and adults in School, Church, Campus, Office and other Fellowships.

Each of the volume is rich with quarterly Bible lessons, stories, drama, songs, seminar, tract materials and a host of other things that can be used to edify, educate, entertains and evangelize every category of people, ranging from children to elderly persons.

Every volume is designed to equip school teachers, ministers in Churches or campus or office fellowships and other people who wish to work with the Lord.

All These And Other Books Are Distributed Worldwide And Published By The Publishing House Of Calvary Rock Resources

*Ikenne-Remo, Nigeria
*Manchester, United Kingdom
*New York, United States

www.calvaryrock.org

www.ingramcontent.com/pod-product-compliance
Lightning Source LLC
Chambersburg PA
CBHW051848040426
42447CB00006B/749